SAIL AND STEAM

Along the Maine Coast

by

VINCENT SHORT AND EDWIN SEARS

The Bond Wheelwright Company

Portland   Maine

To all who still hear the sound of water splashing against the bows of sailing vessels and steamboats, the echo of whistles, the thumping of paddle wheels and propellers while on an ocean voyage Down East.

Acknowledgments

For kind assistance in making this book possible the authors are grateful to:

Mr. Robert B. Applebee, Stockton Springs, Maine

Mr. Charles Henry Powars Copeland, former Curator of Maritime History of the Peabody Museum; now Librarian of the Salem Public Library

Mr. Osgood Williams, Honorary Curator of Steamship History at the Peabody Museum, Salem, Massachusetts

Mr. Harold S. Sniffin, Mariners' Museum, Newport News, Virginia

Professor Evers Burtner, Massachusetts Institute of Technology

Mrs. Elwood W. Leighton, Blue Hill, Maine

Mr. Edwin A. Patt, Executive Secretary, Steamship Historical Society of America

Miss Berla Short, St. Stephen, New Brunswick, Canada

Mr. C. S. Livingston, Red Beach, Maine

Mr. Warren Hathaway Butler, Biddeford Pool, Maine

Mr. George Frederick McRoberts, St. Andrews, New Brunswick

Mr. George MacBeath, St. John, New Brunswick

Mrs. Rose McMahon of Freeport, Maine

Mr. Philip Von Saltza of Salem, Massachusetts

Mr. Frank E. Claes of Camden, Maine
and

Mr. and Mrs. Bond Wheelwright of Freeport, Maine

Their untiring patience and active cooperation have made this first volume of a projected series a reality.

FOREWORD

WHY WE DECIDED TO DO THE BOOKS CALLED
SAIL AND STEAM

Most every inhabitant of the coastal towns or the river ports of New England has an inherent interest in the merchant sailing vessels and steamboats of the old days. My interest started at a very early age when I watched many picturesque schooners, small steamboats, and tugboats sail along the winding St. Croix River, "way Down East."

As shipbuilding and shipping on the river had gradually come to an end, my family moved to Hingham, Massachusetts, where the earliest of the St. Croix steamboats had come from. We started the exciting voyage en route to Hingham on the steamboat *Henry F. Eaton* which steamed down the river from Calais to Eastport, Maine, where we boarded the steamship *Governor Dingley*. Of course it would not occur to any seafaring family like ours to travel by railroad, so we children had the fun of taking an ocean voyage on what then seemed to be a large white ocean liner. This passage was a most memorable event as it was a very rough one indeed; the *Governor Dingley* was known to be somewhat top-heavy, and it rolled so incessantly that we were heaved into forty-five degree positions all night long. We all seemed to be quite good sailors, however, and by the time we reached Boston Harbor my interest in steamboats had increased immeasurably, by leaps and bounds. The continuation of the trip to our new home in Hingham on the steamboat *Betty Alden* from Boston provided additional interest and fascination as I watched schooners, steamboats, tugboats, ferry boats, and ocean-going liners sailing down Boston Harbor.

My father, being an engineer, was especially interested in the history of the steamboat and the full development of its steam engine. His library on steam navigation was rare, and I learned from him that the first two steamboats which ventured out to Nantucket Island and from Boston to Hingham and Salem later paddled their way to Calais,

Maine, and further on to St. John, New Brunswick. I was one of the few, apparently, to learn about these small steamboats, and became so interested by the paintings of these fascinating little steamers which later came into my possession, that I drove my Model T car to Woods Hole to take the ocean voyage to Nantucket Island on the steamboat *Gay Head* which followed part of the route made by the pioneer steamboat *Eagle* in 1818, on the one hundredth anniversary of its first voyage.

The summer of 1918 was the first year that automobiles were admitted to Nantucket, and as a guest of the owner of the first car I was able to see all of this enchanting place during my visit. My first Nantucket Sound steamboat voyage proved to be just the beginning of many more delightful trips. During the summer of 1925 my friend, Edwin Sears, appeared on the Island and made many lovely drawings of historical scenes and places there; he was just as interested in the old steamboats as I was and made charming drawings of the first three little steamers to the Island, the *Eagle, Lafayette,* and *Telegraph,* which are now in the collection at Camden, Maine. I mentioned at that time that the first two little boats had paddled the Maine coast to Calais, my home town, but we could not find any records to prove that my statement was correct or that the steamboat *General Lincoln* had ever towed whale ships into Nantucket Harbor; so we dropped our interest for the time being. My summer holidays were spent at St. Andrews, later on at Gloucester, Massachusetts; then came war service and defense work. Sears continued his summers on Cape Cod, painting and sketching, with frequent trips down east on various steamships, and later acquired the old Cushing Mansion at Camden, Maine. The house had once belonged to the Honorable Edward Cushing who came from a well-known Hingham family, and was one of the incorporators and at one time general manager of the Portland, Bangor and Machias Steamboat Line. His house seemed to be just the proper setting for family heirlooms and our collection of sailing vessel and steamboat paintings which show so clearly the development of the steamboat in this country.

During a conversation with one of our friends, a member of the Steamship Historical Society of America, we developed the idea of a series of books illustrating a continuous growth and progress in steamboat construction, also including a number of the contemporary sailing vessels. We thought it would be interesting to compile the history of each boat and add the story of the development of the marine engine which was as familiar to us as the history of the sailing vessel. First of all, to start these books we would have to make sure that the little boats *Eagle* and *Lafayette* did paddle the Maine Coast to Canada. After visiting Calais, Maine, again, we proved that our history was correct and recorded this essential information never before published. This furnished us inspiration and gave a strong impetus to our writings, and thus the narrative of this history gradually began to take shape. We were long familiar, not only with Maine coast-Boston Harbor steamboats, but also the old Providence, Fall River-New York, Cape Cod canal boats, which were our favorite mode of travel during these times. We have included many portraits of these boats, most of which have long since vanished, for they not only illustrate the development of steam navigation but also compose a picture gallery in book form of various steamers, some of which we sincerely hope will take you on more than one reminiscent voyage along the coast into the harbors and bays of Maine and New Brunswick, or out across the Atlantic and around the world under both Sail and Steam.

Vincent Short

A number of the early inventors who experimented with paddle wheels and propellers—both in Europe and America—from 1452 to 1836, are as follows:

Leonardo Da Vinci	1452
Blasco de Garray	1543
David Ramseye	1630
Salomon de Carrs	1641
Marquis of Worcester	1663
Denis Papin	1690
Thomas Savary	1698
M. Dugnet	1699
Johnathan Hulls	1736
Gautoir	1752
David Bournoulli	1753
Euler	1753
M. Gautier	1756
M. Geneyois	1759
Comtede Auxiron	1774
Perrier	1775
Andrew Ellicott	1775
Guyon de la Plombiere	1776
M. Ducrest	1777
Marquis de Jouffroy	1778
Thomas Paine	1778
Matthew Washbrough	1779
Abbe Darical	1782
James Rumsey	1784-88
William Bushnell (first propeller boat)	1784
Joseph Bramah	1785
John Fitch	1786
Oliver Evan	1788
Nathan Read, Salem, Massachusetts	1788
Patric Millar	1788
William Symington	1788

William Longstreet	1790
John C. Stevens	1791
Baron Seguier	1792
Earl Stanhope	1792
Elijah Ormsbee	1792-96
William Littleton	1794
Samuel Morey	1794
Edward Thompson	1796
Livingston, Stevens, and Roosevelt	1800
Hunter and Dickinson	1800
Edward Shorter	1800
Samuel Brown	1800
Robert Fulton (French experiments)	1802-04
Oliver Evans	1802
Stevens	1804
Robert Fulton	1807
Jonathan Nichols	1807
Robert L. Stevens	1808
John C. Stevens	1809
Fulton Patent	1811
Henry Bell (*Comet*)	1812
Trevatheniet's Patent (propeller vessels in England)	1815
Johnathan Morgan, Wiscasset, Maine	1816

Captain John Ericsson did not obtain a patent for his spiral propeller, which was the first successful propeller invention, until 1836.

CONTENTS

Introduction   1

Our Seafaring Heritage   11

Sails Along the Maine Coast   13

Charles Short   89

America's First Steamboat   95

Maine, New Brunswick and Nova Scotia
      Steamboats and Steamships   99

A Steamboat Voyage Down East   101

Steamboats   105

Appendix   197

LIST OF ILLUSTRATIONS

CHINESE JUNK	facing page 3
DA VINCI DESIGN	7
CROSS HEAD TYPE OF ENGINE	7
THE BEAM ENGINE	9
CAMDEN HARBOR	11
Calais	15
Tam O'Shanter	17
Benjamin Howard	19
Marco Polo	21
Western Continent	23
Red Jacket	25
Fille de l'Air	27
Sea Gem	29
Talisman	31
Ivanhoe	33
Northern Chief	35
Philip Fitzpatrick	37
Emma and Alice	39
Annie H. Smith	41
Wandering Jew	45
Chipman	47
Rocklands	49
George Stetson	on page 51
Jesse H. Freeman	facing page 53
Benjamin F. Packard	55
Morning Star	59
Frederick Billings	61
Annie C. Maguire	65
Governor Ames	67
Henry B. Hyde	69
Jonathan Bourne	on page 73
Shenandoah	facing page 75
George W. Wells	79
Eleanor M. Williams	81
Dorothy Palmer	83

Wyoming facing page 85

Winfield S. Schuster 87

Mr. Charles Short 89

St. Croix Island 91

John Fitch's Boat 95

Clermont 97

Advertisement for Boston and Bangor Line 99

Advertisements for Portland, Yarmouth and
    Eastern Steamship Companies 101

Eagle 105

Savannah 109

Lafayette 111

Bangor 113

Portland I 115

John W. Richmond 117

Penobscot I and Kennebec II 119

T. F. Secor 121

State of Maine II on page 123

Ocean facing page 125

Daniel Webster 127

Forest City 129

Menemon Sanford 131

John Brooks 133

Penobscot II 135

Golden Rod 137

Adelaide 139

City of Portland 141

Kearsarge 143

Rose Standish 145

Katahdin 147

Sagadahoc 149

Cumberland 151

Longfellow 153

Tremont 155

Dirigo 157

Mount Desert 159

Kennebec III 161

Cottage City 163

Portland II   facing page 165
BANGOR, MAINE   167
Frank Jones   169
Vinal Haven   171
Catherine   173
City of Bangor   on page 174
Governor Dingley   facing page 177
Horatio Hall   179
Henry F. Eaton   181
City of Rockland   on page 183
J. T. Morse   facing page 185
Governor Cobb   187
Bunker Hill   189
Camden   191
Rangeley   on page 193
Yarmouth   facing page 195

INTRODUCTION

The day of the merchant sailing vessel and steamboat in coastal New England has nearly drawn to a close, and it is believed that this gathering of portraits and historical data will be of some interest to the lovers and future historians of our old coastal sea-ways.

The compilers are both connected with families which were active in nineteenth-century shipbuilding in Massachusetts, Maine, and New Brunswick, and thus, fortunately, are able to present a number of portraits which have never before been published. Many of these are of New England origin.

Modern modes of travel will never quite efface the memories—still fresh to many—of the most beautiful fleet of steamboats and steamships on the Atlantic Coast which made overnight trips out of Boston, stopping at Portland, Rockland, Camden, Belfast, and Eastport, then going across the Bay of Fundy to St. John.

The handsome *Governor Dingley,* the *Camden,* or the *Belfast* of the Eastern Steamship Line lured many a traveler through the fuss and congestion of Boston's Atlantic Avenue, with its biting aroma of hemp and roasting coffee, fish, and clean sea air, and up their sparkling gangways to the bracing hours ahead of an ocean voyage of one hundred sea miles. The coast of Maine rose austerely off the port bow; the distance across the bounding deep to Land's End and the English Channel was scarcely more than the length of the shoreline to Eastport which was marked with splendid harbors, lighthouses, and full cargoes waiting to be moved from the wharves.

Those years have been described as "the gay and delightful era of steamboating"; but to talk of them at the beginning of this book is to start the story near its end. Quickly we may see the long history of Maine ships reach back to 1607, when the pinnace *Virginia* was built. But . . . to search for the real beginning of shipbuilding, the first successful sailing vessels of the world, and the earliest known methods of navigation, we turn to southeastern Asia and China, for we know that the Chinese knew how to sail the ocean hundreds of years before Columbus' famous voyages.

1

The Chinese junk, very simply designed and lightly constructed, with sails made of straw matting, was able to make voyages around the world in safety and comfort. An eye was sometimes painted on each side of the bow of the vessel, and tradition states that the Chinese felt that this would enable the vessel to see, and help it to reach its destination. The straw-matted sails resembled the fins of a fish and caught a light breeze very easily.

Marco Polo was familiar with these Chinese vessels and traveled from China to Italy in a junk more than seven centuries ago. He considered these vessels more practical than the contemporary European-built ships, as they were built with two water-tight compartments fore and aft which made them practically unsinkable; they were moderately clean, well ventilated, comfortable, and seaworthy in every respect.

The evolution from sail to steam, with the transitional combinations of both, can be seen in the pages to follow. These significant changes took place only after a number of false starts.

Blasco de Garray, a native of Biscay, Spain, in 1543 successfully built a vessel called the *Trinity,* equipped with steam and paddle wheels, but his invention was so ridiculed that he was forced to abandon it. Later he built another successful steamboat, was rewarded by Charles the Fifth, and made a naval officer. However, the emperor was finally persuaded by advisers that the project was not only dangerous but of little practical use. Few of the details of this early experiment have come down to us.

It is not impossible that some of the early experiments with paddlewheels were influenced by a knowledge of Leonardo da Vinci's design for a self-propelled vessel.

The story of the steamboat in America began along the shores of the Delaware River after the independence of the country was assured. The air was full of projects and at the same time that tenuous beginnings were made in scientific investigation, John Fitch obtained from several state legislatures the exclusive right, for fourteen years, to build and operate steamboats on the waters of these states. Having built several successful models, he enlisted the aid of prominent Philadelphians, whose financial backing enabled him to start work on a 45-foot boat.

The vessel was finally launched and successfully operated on the Delaware River at Philadelphia on August 22, 1787. It was propelled by a series of twelve paddles—six to a side, arranged like those of an Indian war canoe—and operated by steam power. Although Fitch constructed four successful steamboats he failed to see the need for

3

demonstrating the economical aspects of steam navigation, and accordingly lost all financial support.

In 1789, Nathan Read of Salem and Danvers, Massachusetts, later of Belfast, Maine, constructed a manually operated paddlewheel boat, which he planned to use with his improved double-acting steam engine, but was unable to secure financial assistance in building a full-size steamboat.

Three years later, in 1792, Elijah Ormsbee pulled the throttle on his successful experimental craft at Windsor's Cove, now East Providence, Rhode Island.

Edward Shorter was the first to experiment in this country with a propeller-driven craft, about 1800, but the propeller did not come into general use until the mid-century.

In 1816, Jonathan Morgan, Esq., of Wiscasset, Maine, formerly of Portland, designed and built a flat-bottomed boat of about 50 tons, which he named the *Alpha;* he invented and built a steam engine of the propeller type to go in it.

The boiler, made of hard pine, was about the size of a regular tar barrel and into it was fixed a fire box of iron. A chain connected the engine with the propeller.

Morgan anticipated making a fortune with his invention. He took the *Alpha* on a trip up the Kennebec River, and did this under great difficulty, as the engine had barely enough power to steam the current. He did gain headway and went as far as Augusta.

After the boat returned to Wiscasset, it was not considered a success, and Mr. Morgan was reputed to be an eccentric citizen, as was the case with many inventors and geniuses of his time. With some help and encouragement, no doubt, his little steamer could have been improved.

The vessel was sold at public auction, the machinery was removed, and the boat was made into a fishing vessel. Mr. Morgan moved back to Portland, and both he and the *Alpha* were soon forgotten.

The steamboat era really began, however, with Robert Fulton. His *Clermont,* built by Charles Brown, a well-known New York shipbuilder, was 133 feet long, 7 deep and 18 feet broad. A Watt steam-engine, especially built in England, was placed in the forward part of the boat and left open to view. Back of it was a 20-foot boiler set in brickwork and housed over. The boat was propelled by two side paddle wheels, 15 feet in diameter.

The *Clermont* began her memorable voyage up the Hudson from New York to Albany on August 17, 1807. The round trip took five days, but the vessel was under way only sixty-two hours, with an average speed of almost five miles an hour.

John Ericsson, a Swedish engineer, was pre-eminent in the development of the screw propeller, although the principle had been more or less fully realized since the seventeenth century. Ericsson came from England to the United States in 1839, and by 1844 there were in use some twenty-five vessels with screw propellers.

The first steamboat to enter Salem and Boston harbors was the *Massachusetts*. Two other early steamboats were the *Eagle* and the *Lafayette*, these being the first to travel from New Bedford to Nantucket, and later to act as the first steamers on the Boston to Hingham run. They were eventually transferred to the Calais and Eastport, Maine, region, where they were the first known steamboats in eastern Maine, the pioneers of a long succession to come to the Maine coast from Massachusetts.

New Bedford and Nantucket were the first places in the United States to experiment with steamboats as a practical means of service, and theirs is the first steamboat line still in continuous use. The following sailing vessel and steamboat portraits are those of the New England and New Brunswick coast, with other portraits of vessels that contributed much to the early development of the sailing vessel and steam navigation.

Vincent Short
Edwin Sears

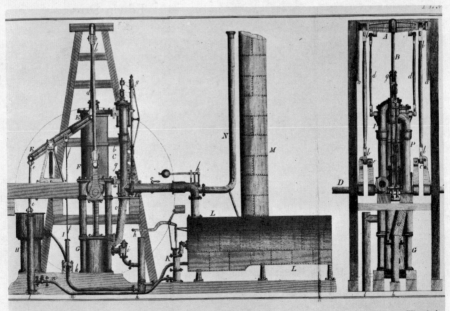

Leonardo da Vinci's design for a self-propelled ship which he hoped would be navigated by mechanical means. The origin of the stern paddlewheel boat has been attributed to the Chinese, whereas the origin of paddle wheels placed on both sides of a vessel has been attributed to Leonardo da Vinci.

Cross Head Type of Engine

This type of steam engine was the kind of engine used on most of the early flat-bottomed steamboats paddling the Gulf of Maine, including steamboats *Bangor I* and *Portland I*.

A cross head engine was one with a beam or bar across the head or end of the rod, attached by a knuckle pin especially to the solid cross piece running between parallel sides which received motion from the piston of the steam engine and imparted it to the connecting rod.

This kind of engine was the first really successful type used on coast and river steamboats in this country.

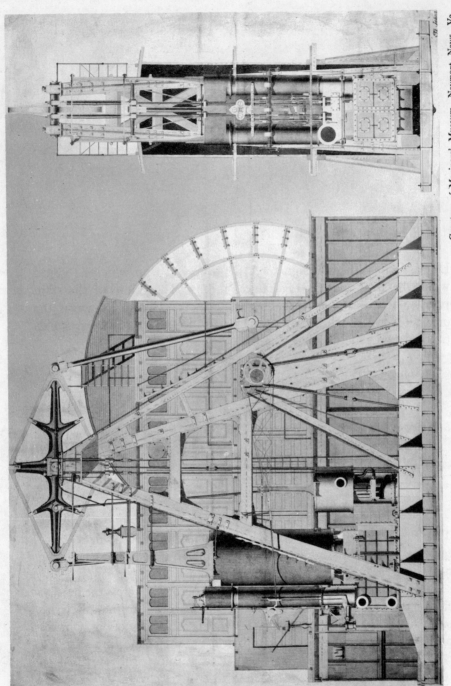

The Beam Engine

This type of engine, often called the walking beam, was used on many of the flat-bottomed Maine coast and river steamboats and was one with a vibrating beam through which the piston effort was transmitted to the crank, or its equivalent; in distinction from one having its piston rod attached directly to the connecting rod which turned the crank and paddle wheels.

Steamboats *City of Bangor, City of Rockland, Penobscot, Bay State, The Portland* and others were equipped with this type of engine.

CAMDEN HARBOR

From the earliest Colonial days shipbuilding has been the most interesting of all industries. The small vessel *Virginia* built at Popham, Maine, in 1607 was the earliest one known to have been built on the New England coast, and it is said that this vessel made several transAtlantic voyages to England.

Among the earliest shipbuilding records of the Passamaquoddy Region is that of a schooner which was named *First Attempt,* built by Mr. Thomas Vose at Robbinston, Maine, in 1792. Mr. Vose built a number of ships after that time, both at Robbinston and St. Andrews, New Brunswick. His shipyards were the earliest ones in operation at Robbinston.

Mr. Thomas Vose was born at Milton, Massachusetts, and moved to Robbinston, Maine, in 1790; he passed on at Robbinston, on November 13, 1848. Some of the woodlands once owned by him, including Vose Lake, lie southwest of Calais, Maine. It was near this location that the twelve large trees were cut for the columns of the beautiful Bulfinch State House at Boston, when Maine and Massachusetts were one state.

After the War of 1812, the rights of American ships and seamen were more firmly established and shipbuilding was again started with great strength and enterprise all along the coast of New England and New Brunswick.

There was a very gradual development or improvement in the designing and building of sailing vessels from the year 1815 to 1850.

In 1834, Lloyd's of London established the Registry of Shipping for the proper survey and classification of all merchant ships of Great Britain. The American Shipmasters' Association established a record of both American and foreign shipping in 1867.

In 1832, the fast vessel *Ann McKim* was built at Baltimore, Maryland. In 1842, the swift ship *Courier* was built at East Boston, Massachusetts, by Donald McKay and was the first really fast vessel built by this master shipbuilder who later became world famous for his speedy ships known as "clippers."

At Saint John, New Brunswick, the magnificent ship *Marco Polo* was built in 1851, and the great ship *Flying Cloud* was built at East Boston during the same year; the *Marco Polo* was an entirely different type of vessel but was equally as fine and beautiful in very different ways.

11

In 1852, the famous New England sea captain Daniel C. Bacon became President of The American Navigation Club and challenged the shipbuilders of Great Britain, which speeded all sailing ships from port to port. Many of the most competent, capable, and hard driving of the sea captains who commanded the fast so-called clippers came from Brewster, Massachusetts, on Cape Cod. In 1853, Captain Frederic Howes of Brewster invented and perfected the double topsails used on all clipper ships, also other sails, used on many of the ships, which made record passages and voyages possible. Later sails were cut down considerably; but fast voyages continued as the designing of both vessels and sails greatly improved.

One of the largest of ships built during this period was the *Break of Day* built by James Porter of Calais, Maine, in 1853; this was not one of the fastest ships of its time but a very fine one.

In 1855, the medium clipper ship *Andrew Jackson* built at Mystic, Connecticut, made the record New York-San Francisco passage and was probably the fastest New York-San Francisco clipper type ship. The sails invented by Captain Howes were used on this vessel.

In 1864, the barque *Sea Gem,* one of the smaller vessels built by J. & C. Short at St. Stephen, New Brunswick, Canada, made a record passage to Liverpool.

American and Canadian built wooden sailing vessels exceeded those of all foreign countries in classification, endurance, and beauty. The ship *Marco Polo* was probably the fastest sailing ship in the world. The so-called Down Easters followed the clipper ships and the clipper type barques. These vessels were the most outstanding in maritime history. Last of all sailing vessels to remain in merchant service were the coastal schooners; the word "schoon" originated with the Dutch, meaning to schoon or sail. The first vessel of this type built in this country was built by Andrew Robinson, a Scotchman, at Gloucester, Massachusetts, in 1715, and at the close of the clipper-ship era the schooners held a very important place in the shipping world; they were used in large numbers along our coast, and many also found their way to foreign ports.

Though the steamboat was first perfected in America, builders of wooden sailing ships continued to build long after the development of steam navigation, as many of these vessels made faster passages than the steamships of the time, especially the Down Easters which were less expensive to sail. Then came the perfected marine engine, overland transportation, and the end of the merchant sailing vessel era. Schooners continued in service along the New England coast until about 1920.

12

SAIL AND STEAM ALONG THE MAINE COAST

Brig   *Calais*

Built in 1841   Captain Francis Deming, 1843
Captain Thomas Rogers, 1841   Captain Harrison Klein, 1845

The *Calais,* named for the once famous lumber mart city on the St. Croix River, was built by the Messrs. Joshua Briggs and J. N. M. Brewer. The firm was known as Briggs & Brewer and had shipyards located on both sides of the river at Robbinston, Maine, and Brandy Cove near St. Andrews, New Brunswick. The brig *Calais* was built and launched from their shipyards at Robbinston on September 10, 1841, and after the vessel was fully rigged it was enrolled at Passamaquoddy, now Eastport, Maine.

This vessel was unusual in design, having a heavy but handsomely carved and gilded billet head and square stern, and its heavy bowsprit was placed well inside the bluff bow. Some of these early vessels were considered cumbersome and heavy because they were planked with white oak from the keel to just above the water line and sometimes coppered.

The *Calais* was owned by Mr. George Gates, Martha Gates of Robbinston, Maine, Samuel Pike, and Edward A. Barnard of Calais, Maine. This portrait was probably painted at the port of Marseilles, as this vessel made several transatlantic voyages and was later sold to foreign interests.

Other vessels built by Briggs & Brewer were the ships *Gossipian, Lord Ashburton, Abbotsford, Rothschild, Birkenhead, Julius Caesar, Alexander Grant;* the barques *Isabella Stewart, Lady Sarah Bailey, Catharine, Annie Armstrong, Sarah Marks;* the brig *Hibernia,* and the schooner *Challenger.* After the Messrs. Briggs and Brewer had passed on, the business was carried on by Mrs. Brewer, and she is probably the only known lady shipbuilder. The Brewer Mansion at Robbinston, Maine, is one of the most beautiful houses of the St. Croix region.

The *Calais* was 86 feet long,
21 feet breadth, 9 feet depth of hold;
149 tons.

15

Ship

Tam O' Shanter

Built in 1874

Captains: Captains:
  Horace Soule, 1874-79   Waite
  Charles Dumond Prescott, 1879-86   Ballard
  Peabody, 1891-99

The ship *Tam O' Shanter,* first by name, was built by Enos Soule at Freeport, Maine, in 1842. This vessel was 176 feet long, 34 feet breadth, and 16 feet depth of hold, 977 tons, and adorned with a billet head and square stern.

Another member of the Soule family, Enos C. Soule of Freeport, Maine, was the commander who sailed this vessel for California from Boston on November 15, 1853, with eleven passengers and a full cargo; Captain Soule did not arrive at San Francisco until about four months later, entering the Golden Gate on March 25, 1853; he continued to Calcutta, and on the return voyage to Boston, the *Tam O' Shanter* foundered off Cape Cod in December of that year; the vessel is said to have been heavy and cumbersome.

The Soule family built another ship at Freeport in 1874 which they also named *Tam O' Shanter,* and this vessel's bow also terminated with a billet head, its stern was square, and like most of the ships built by the Soules, it was heavy and strong as iron, with excellent cargo capacity. *Tam O' Shanter* was a very handsome ship under sail and proved to be a fast and seaworthy vessel. The fastest passage known to have been made was while racing the big four-masted barque *Shenendoah* to the Golden Gate; the *Tam O' Shanter* won this race, the *Shenendoah* having been delayed by fog just outside of the harbor. This ship made many successful crossings to Liverpool, also survived several hazardous voyages around the Horn to San Francisco and China; one passage to San Francisco was made in 119 days and another in 122 days.

In 1899, this ship was sold to an oil company and foundered while on a voyage to Hong Kong.

The *Tam O' Shanter* was 213 feet long, 41 feet breadth, 24 feet depth of hold; 1,602 tons.

17

Ship

Benjamin Howard
Built in 1851
Captain James Stackpole

The *Benjamin Howard* was built at Camden, Maine, by Carleton, Norwood & Company, who also had shipyards at Rockport, Maine.

This vessel was designed and built with a billet head and square stern. In merchant sailing vessel registers the *Benjamin Howard* was listed as a clipper ship.

The original owners were J. G. Norwood, Philander J. Carleton, and S. D. Carleton, all of Camden, Maine. Later the vessel was sold in Norway, and again sold and registered from Copenhagen in 1864.

The *Benjamin Howard* was 150 feet long, 31 feet breadth, 15 feet depth of hold; 650 tons.

Marco Polo

Launched April 17, 1851
Captain James Nichols "Bully" Forbes

The *Marco Polo,* the most celebrated of all Canadian built ships, was built as a regular timber ship and became known as a clipper packet with a reputation as the fastest in the world. This vessel was built by James Smith of Saint John with three decks and a half-poop, and at the time of the launching was the largest vessel laid down by any local shipbuilder up to that time.

Fame didn't come immediatly. The ship sailed from Saint John to Liverpool in fifteen days, then to Mobile, Alabama, and back again to Liverpool, before the vessel caught the eye of an Irish speculator, Paddy McGee, who bought the ship and then sold it to James Baines, head of the new Australian Black Ball Line.

Baines refitted the vessel, sheathed the hull in copper, and then placed the ship in emigrant trade between Liverpool and Melbourne, Australia. The stern board on the square stern represented a carved elephant and two reclining figures of Marco Polo, one in European dress, the other in Oriental garb, making the stern one of exceptional beauty. The figurehead was a full-length figure, also representing the renowned explorer.

The vessel sailed for Australia in July 1852 under the command of Captain James "Bully" Forbes, one of the most colorful sea captains of the British Merchant Marine. Aboard were nine hundred and fifty passengers, a crew of thirty and thirty others working their passage. The trip usually took between 100 and 120 days. The *Marco Polo* made the passage in 68 days and the return trip in 74 days.

The *Marco Polo* and Forbes were the talk of the shipping world, and on a large strip of canvas between the ship's fore and mainmasts, this vessel was proclaimed "The Fastest Ship in the World."

The ship was beached at Cape Cavendish, Prince Edward Island, on July 22, 1883, after leaking badly in a storm. The hull later fell to pieces, but many of the carvings and relics from the ship were saved. One of the famous carved figures may be seen in the Saint John Museum, at Saint John, New Brunswick, Canada.

> The *Marco Polo* was 184 feet long;
> 36 feet breadth, 29 feet depth of hold;
> 1,622 tons.

Clipper Ship **Western Continent**

Built in 1853
Captain Stephen Higgins

The *Western Continent* was a full model sailing ship with billet head and square stern, built by H. E. Carter at Pembroke, Maine, for John M. Mayo of Boston.

This superb portrait was painted by a Chinese artist in Hong Kong Harbor in 1858.

The ship was sold to Robert C. Hopper, Boston, in 1854, and in 1867 the vessel was owned by Bates & Company of Boston.

The *Western Continent* made many voyages from Boston and New York to San Francisco, Hong Kong, Singapore, Bangkok, Rio de Janeiro, and other foreign ports; two of the sailings have been recorded as follows: 1854-1855, New York to San Francisco in 121 days; 1856-1857, New York to San Francisco, Valparaiso, Manila, and back to Boston in 176 days. The ship also made voyages to Falmouth, London, and Liverpool. The last recorded voyage in 1866 was to San Francisco.

The *Western Continent* was 198 feet long, 37 feet breadth, 21 feet depth of hold; 1,222 tons.

Clipper Ship   *Red Jacket*

Launched in 1853
Captain Asa Eldridge
Captain Samuel Reid

The *Red Jacket* was considered the handsomest vessel to be launched by American builders, an extreme clipper ship, the most beautiful ever constructed in Maine. Built by George Thomas of Rockland, Maine, the slender, graceful frame was moulded by Samuel H. Pook of Boston, the builder of the famous ship *Game Cock*. Designed with three decks, it had fourteen staterooms, cabins beautifully panelled in mahogany and other choice woods, and luxurious furnishings. It was named after a noted Seneca Indian of the Wolf Clan, Chief Sagoyewatha, "He Who Keeps Them Awake," conspicuous for the brilliant red jacket he wore, which was presented to him by a British officer during the American Revolution when he espoused the cause of Great Britain. He was represented in the exquisitely carved, life-sized figurehead; the carved and gilded stern piece represented an old Indian chief.

This superb water color portrait shows the vessel coasting, probably in Long Island Sound near New York, where, after the launching on November 2, 1853, the *Red Jacket* was towed for rigging and sailmaking, everything perfectly proportioned to the finely moulded hull.

Captain Asa Eldridge of Yarmouth, Cape Cod, was given command of the *Red Jacket;* he was an expert navigator and seaman, internationally known. The maiden voyage began on January 10, 1854, from New York to Liverpool, with a crew of sixty-three men. This was a record voyage through continuous storms, made from dock to dock in thirteen days, one hour, and twenty-five minutes, which stands as the fastest record any clipper ship ever made on this run.

The ship was immediately chartered for a voyage to Melbourne under the command of Captain Samuel Reid; and sailed back from Melbourne with passengers and a cargo of gold dust valued at £2,000,000 sterling. On arrival the vessel was purchased by Pilkington & Wilson for passenger service in their White Star Line to Australia.

In 1868 the ship was sold to Wilson and Chambers of Liverpool and placed in the timber trade between London and Quebec. Then, like many other sailing vessels, after a most successful career, the *Red Jacket* ended its days as a coal barge, at Cape Verde.

The *Red Jacket* was 251 feet long,
44 feet breadth, 31 feet depth of hold;
2,306 tons uncoppered.

Barque

Fille de L'Air

Built in 1863
Captain J. Williams

The *Fille de l'Air* was designed and built at St. Stephen, New Brunswick, in 1863 by Messrs. John and Charles Short.

This vessel, with a female figurehead and round stern, is said to have been built with the speediest lines of any barque constructed on the Atlantic Coast, the plans being laid down by the best English marine architects and builders of the time.

Rumor has it that the *Fille de l'Air* was built as a blockade runner for the United States, but there is no record to show that this barque was used for any purpose other than legitimate trade.

The vessel was sold to J. S. De Wolf and Company of Liverpool in 1871.

The *Fille de l'Air* was 184 feet long, 24.8 feet breadth, 13.7 feet depth of hold; 1,416 tons.

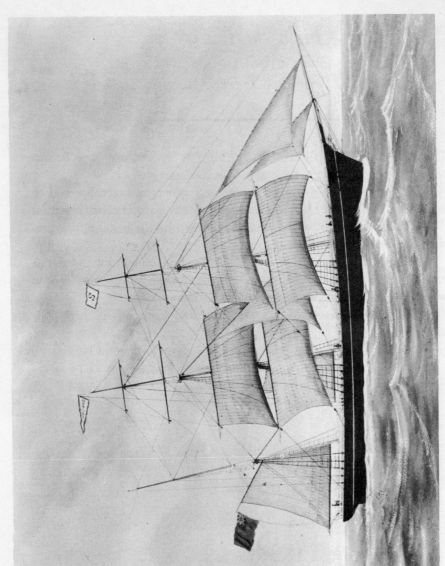

Barque   *Sea Gem*

Launched in 1864
Captain J. Pettingrew
Captain E. R. Fax
Captain O. Tollefsen

The *Sea Gem* was built at St. Stephen, New Brunswick, by Messrs. John and Charles Short, and launched on April 23, 1864. Registered at St. Andrews, New Brunswick, the owners were J. & C. Short, and Chipman & Company.

This barque, with a female figurehead and round stern, was most appropriately named. Though one of the smallest vessels built by the Messrs. Short at their St. Stephen yards, the *Sea Gem* received one of the highest ratings ever given by Lloyd's of London.

This portrait shows the vessel making speed with very little sail at a time when the wind was strong and favorable.

The *Sea Gem* made one of the fastest sailings across the Atlantic Ocean on record for a barque of comparable size, having sailed from The Ledge on the St. Croix River to Liverpool in fourteen days, even though the voyage was made during the summer months when the winds were light and variable.

The vessel was sold in Norway on May 11, 1875, and renamed *Axel*. The signal letters were H. J. K. L. In all, she was in service over thirty years; made many voyages to Liverpool, New York, and Helsingburg.

> The *Sea Gem* was 148 feet long,
> 31 feet breadth, 18 feet depth of hold;
> 575 tons.

Ship   *Talisman*

Launched in 1864
Captain J. Cragie
Captain D. Thomas

The *Talisman* was built at St. Stephen, New Brunswick, by Messrs. John and Charles Short in 1864 for Chipman & Company. The ship was registered at St. Andrews, and was one of the finest vessels built by these celebrated designers and builders, receiving an exceptionally high rating from Lloyd's of London.

This portrait shows the *Talisman* outward bound from Passamaquoddy Bay en route to St. John after the rigging had been completed at The Ledge on the St. Croix River. Many of the vessels built on the St. Croix sailed to St. John for a cargo before proceeding to England, Norway, and France. As can be seen, the captain has the port studding sails set, but not the starboard, so that the ship is not sailing entirely before the wind.

The ship was sold to William Milligan & Company at Liverpool in 1865, and later made many transatlantic voyages around Cape Horn to San Francisco. The *Talisman* was still sailing the ocean in 1893, being surveyed in San Francisco in that year. Signal letters were W. Q. F. M.

The *Talisman* was 213 feet long,
35 feet breadth, 22 feet depth of hold;
1,026 tons.

Ship   *Ivanhoe*

Built in 1865
Captain F. Horace Harriman
Captain Albert Harriman

The *Ivanhoe* was built at Belfast, Maine, in 1865, in the yards of C. R. Carter & Company, for Paul R. Hazeltine, of Belfast, and certain of his neighbors.

This merchant ship was engaged in the general carrying trade, chiefly to ports in South America. On one voyage from Boston to San Francisco, in 1869, the cargo was valued at $40,734.00.

Soon after Captain Albert Harriman left her in 1884, the *Ivanhoe* was sold by the Maine owners to the Black Diamond Coal Company of San Francisco for use in the coastwise coal trade.

The ship was lost with all hands in a hurricane off Cape Flattery on September 29, 1894. Signal letters were H. K. J. C.

The *Ivanhoe* was 202 feet long, 40 feet breadth, 27 feet depth of hold; 1,610 tons.

Barque

Northern Chief

Built in 1872
Captain Homer
Captain D. Millar, 1879

The *Northern Chief* was one of the later vessels designed and built by the Messrs. John and Charles Short at their St. Stephen yards; these gentlemen were the sole owners when the vessel was completed.

This staunchly constructed barque is said to have been towed to St. John to be rigged, but was more probably rigged and fitted out at The Ledge on the St. Croix River, where most of the vessels of that period built at the St. Stephen yards came for the completion of final details.

This renowned sailing vessel was sold to parties at Yarmouth, England, in 1878, and was later registered at Liverpool in 1885. Its signal letters were M. H. B. Q.

The *Northern Chief* was 176 feet long, 28 feet breadth, 20 feet depth of hold; 803 tons.

Barque   *Philip Fitzpatrick*

Built in 1873
Captain W. Phelan, 1873
Captain Oscar Clark, 1884

The *Philip Fitzpatrick* was built by the Short Brothers in their ship-yards at Calais, Maine, in 1873. The barques built by these shipbuilders had good cargo capacity as well as excellent speed; this clipper type barque was designed with a graceful pointed bow, a beautifully carved billet head, which was often called a fiddle head, also an interestingly carved stern piece.

The vessel was first owned by Philip Fitzpatrick of Philadelphia, where it was registered; it was later registered at New York. In 1886, Calais was the home port. Jonathan Ross was the last owner, in 1888. The signal letters were J. N. V. L.

This unusual photograph shows the *Philip Fitzpatrick* at a location on the St. Croix River, just below St. Stephen, New Brunswick, known as The Ledge. The picture was taken just after the rigging had been completed and shows the perfection of this rigging as an exquisite pattern against the sky. The wharves and numerous waterfront buildings at The Ledge have long since disappeared with the passage of time. The Devil's Head on the Calais shoreline appears in the background.

The *Philip Fitzpatrick* was 147 feet long, 32 feet breadth, 17 feet depth of hold; 582 tons.

Barque Emma & Mette. Built by Alex. Rios on the St Croix River, Calais Me. Capt. C.E. Fulton. 1874.

Barque   *Emma and Alice*

Built in 1874
Captain W. C. Gibbs
Captain C. E. Fulton

The clipper type barque with the delightful name of *Emma and Alice* was the last vessel of such design built by the Short Brothers in their own shipyards at Calais, Maine; it was first owned by James Murchie & Sons, the well-known lumber merchants of the St. Croix region, and was probably named for members of the Murchie family.

The *Emma and Alice* was beautifully designed with a graceful clipper bow, a handsomely carved figurehead, finely carved quarterboards and a sternboard placed on the rounded stern; after the launching, the vessel was rigged at The Ledge where the captain took command and loaded the hull with a cargo of lumber for Boston and Nantucket Island, Massachusetts.

As the American and Canadian built sailing vessels continued to be finer and faster than those built in England or Scotland, this vessel was sold in 1876 to MacEachran, Fulton & Kerr of Greenock, Scotland. Captain C. E. Fulton being one of the owners, sailed with a cargo to Scotland. This vessel is said to have ended its days in service among the British Isles.

The portrait of the *Emma and Alice* is a European artist's interpretation, painted in the decorative French manner. The signal letters were J. D. B. W.

> The *Emma and Alice* was 156 feet long, 32 feet breadth, 19 feet depth of hold; 701 tons.

Ship Anna H. Smith of Calais Maine ~ Capt. J. H. Bartlett 1876
Built in Port Blair on the St. Croix River

From the Authors' Collection

Square Rigger ## *Annie H. Smith*

Built in 1876
Captain J. F. Bartlett
Captain R. B. Brown
Captain Charles S. Kendall

The ship *Annie H. Smith* was the last large vessel to be built at Calais, Maine. Ship designers and builders were consolidating in order to continue with the production of sailing ships which were rapidly diminishing from our coasts and rivers. This ship was built by the Short Brothers of St. Stephen, N. B., and Calais, in the Nickerson and Rideout Yards. It was given an exceptionally fine rating, but was the last ship to be built by them at Calais; the firm continued, however, to design and build small vessels and schooners.

This ship was built for F. H. Smith & Company of New York and named after Mr. Smith's daughter who later married the son of the ship's first commander, Captain Bartlett.

The maiden voyage of this vessel was from New York southeastward to Melbourne; it was chartered for £3350 and made a very good passage in seventy-four days, taking a cargo and about three hundred fifty passengers. After the last of the cargo had been discharged at Sidney, this ship sailed from Newcastle to San Francisco in 62 days, then went around the Horn to Liverpool with a cargo of wheat in 118 days, later returning to New York, completing a most successful round-the-world voyage.

After the maiden voyage this vessel sailed in trade, principally to ports in the Far East, making many fast passages from New York to San Francisco; it sometimes crossed the Pacific from the Orient to load California wheat for Europe, making several profitable voyages.

In 1883, the *Annie H. Smith* was commanded by Captain Rowland B. Brown, a native of Castine, Maine, who took his wife and their five children to sea. Later he made a very successful trip from Cardiff to Hong Kong, and no doubt the original portrait of this ship painted by a Chinese artist was done while the ship was on this voyage. The Chinese artist's interpretation of the vessel accounts for the inaccurate detail of the rigging, but it is considered a most artistic painting.

This ship survived a most trying experience during the great blizzard which swept the Atlantic coast in March, 1888, in which many ships were wrecked and others were extensively damaged. The vessel had been towed from New York and dropped anchor in the Chesapeake Bay, preparing to load a cargo for San Francisco, when the terrific storm burst forth. The ship broke away from both anchor chains, but was miraculously brought up with a manila hawser attached to a spare anchor to which the vessel rode successfully until the storm abated three days later.

On one of the ship's westward voyages around Cape Horn it was badly beaten by a storm off the Cape. The sails, rigging, and spars were damaged, the rudder head was twisted off, but the ship made Port Stanley for repairs and soon proceeded to San Francisco.

This clipper type square rigger was one of the first so-called real Down Easters which was the splendid design of men from way Down East and New Brunswick. These Down Easters were considered the most successful of all the wooden sailing vessels, and many of the finest were built in Maine.

Unfortunately the end of the *Annie H. Smith* was a sad one, for after seventeen years as a most serviceable and useful merchant sailing vessel, it was converted into a coal barge and was later rammed and sunk by a steamship along the Atlantic coast.

The well-known Captain Hobart Dodge of Islesboro, Maine, started his career as a cabin boy on board this vessel. The signal letters were J. S. F. H.

> The *Annie H. Smith* was 222 feet long, 40 feet breadth, 24 feet depth of hold; 1,452 tons.

Wandering Jew

Launched in 1877
Captain Henry Talpey
Captain D. E. Nichols

The *Wandering Jew,* second vessel of that name to be built at Camden, Maine, was launched on September 2, 1877, and was considered one of the smartest ships of the American Merchant Marine. This ship was built by the master builder J. Pascal of Camden and Rockport for Carleton, Norwood & Company, and was registered at Searsport, Maine; the signal letters were J. S. N. C.

Like most of the Down East ships, the frame was finely moulded and terminated with a billet head and rounded stern. It had a double deck; above the main deck was a hurricane deck which was all flush fore and aft. It was also built with a crown chamber so that any water that washed on board would run off through the scuppers at once. From the bow to the taffrail, the upper deck was broken by several projections which were the capstan, the fo'c'sle, masts, fife rails, rope coils, scuttles, hatch, cabin skylights, and the wheelhouse. This ship was exceptionally well rigged with a main skysail, and was one of two flush-deck, full-rigged ships built in the United States, neither of which had poop or quarter deck. A forward house furnished accommodations for the crew, carpenter's shop, and galley, etc., while a house aft, sometimes called a caboose, contained cabins, captain's and officers' rooms, and also spare staterooms.

The first voyage of the *Wandering Jew* was to have been made from New York to San Francisco, but a more remunerative freight offer was made, and the vessel took case oil from Philadelphia to Antwerp, making the passage from Camden, Maine, to Philadelphia in 5 days; 25 days thence to Antwerp; 9 days to Cardiff; 118 days thence to Hong Kong; and 33 days from Hong Kong to San Francisco. Up to that time this vessel's daily average while at sea was 134 miles, having sailed by log 25,460 miles; the passage from Hong Kong to San Francisco has never been beaten. From San Francisco to Liverpool a passage was made in 115 days, which established the *Wandering Jew*'s reputation as a fast ship that was maintained to the end.

In 1895, the *Wandering Jew* sailed a memorable race from Hong Kong to New York with the *Tam O' Shanter,* described on page 17. Both ships left Hong Kong on the same day; they met several times

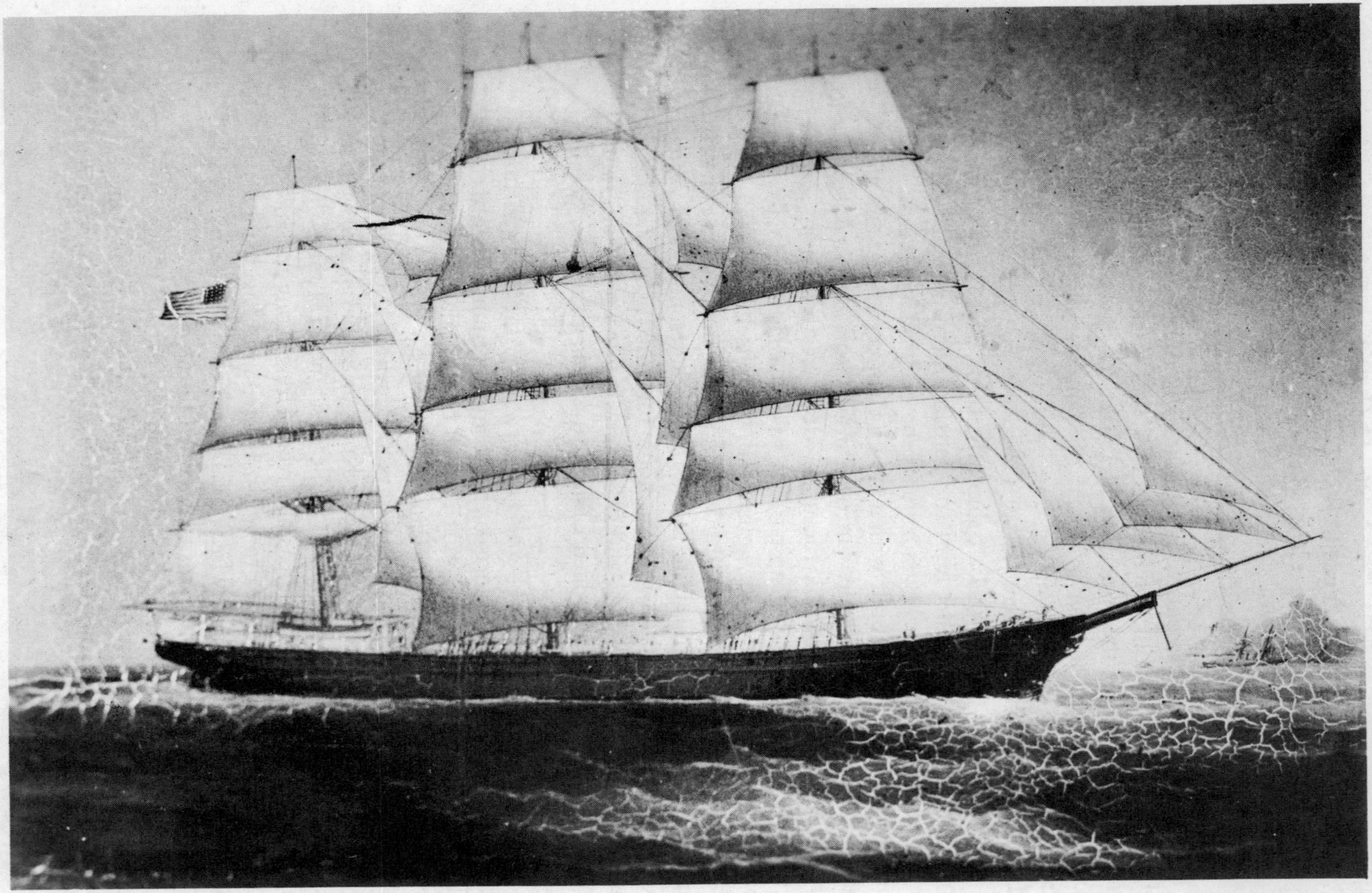

From the Authors' Collection

during the long passage, and entered New York Harbor at the same time. As these ships were well balanced, the race was considered a tie.

The *Wandering Jew* returned to Hong Kong and on October 20, 1895, caught fire and was scuttled. Members of the crew were accused of having started the fire, but this could not be proved at the inquiry. The ship was raised and demasted, the hull was housed over and towed up the river above Shanghai for use as a freight landing barge.

Throughout the entire career of this ship there were only two commanders, Captain Talpey and Captain Nichols. Captain Talpey had sailed for Carleton, Norwood & Company for many years and had commanded the barques *Bertha,* which was lost in the China Sea, *Adelia, Carleton,* and *Samuel D. Carleton,* and the ship *John Pascal*.

Captain Nichols was born at Searsport in 1845 and was the son of a shipbuilder. He went to sea at 15, and at the age of 24 became captain of the barque *Commodore Dupont,* remaining in command for 8 years, and then became commander of the barque *Robert Porter* for 7 years. After the burning of the *Wandering Jew,* Captain Nichols took command of the vessel *Emily Reed* until 1900, and his final command was on board the *Manuel Llanguna* until 1905. From then until the time he passed on at Belfast, Maine, in November, 1928, Captain Nichols managed a woodworking mill at Searsport.

The *Wandering Jew* was engaged principally in trade to the Orient, and in 1880 made a passage around Cape Horn from Liverpool to San Francisco in 131 days. Several good passages were made from San Francisco to India, China, and Japan, and other voyages were made to Hong Kong, Canton, and Singapore.

The *Wandering Jew* was 219 feet long, 40 feet breadth, 29 feet depth of hold; 1737 gross tons and 1660 net tons.

The first ship *Wandering Jew* was originally named *National Eagle* but was renamed before documentation. This vessel was built by Carleton, Norwood & Company at Camden, Maine, in 1853. Captain James Stackpole was the first master; a later command was assumed by Captain C. C. Smart. This ship was designed and built with a figurehead and square stern, being 179 feet long, 37 feet breadth, and 18 feet depth of hold.

The owners were James Stackpole, Carleton, Norwood & Company, Horatio Alden, Blanchard and Sherman, and J. W. Elwell. This vessel made many voyages from New York to San Francisco, Canton, and Hong Kong, and on May 3, 1864, was sold to British interests, renamed *Lotta Maria,* and used on the coast of China from 1866 to 1886.

Ship

Chipman

Built in 1877
Captain John Lewis, First Master
Captain J. Williams
Captain Bugge

The ship *Chipman* was built by the Messrs. Short at their shipyard in St. Stephen, N. B., Canada, in 1877; the firm Chipman & Bolton, and J. & C. Short were the owners. This vessel was of a most graceful design, adorned with a handsome figurehead, white in gold leaf, and beautifully carved and gilded scrollwork on the bow; an interestingly carved stern piece was placed on its rounded stern. The hull of this ship was of most unusual construction having diagonal planking on the sides. It was painted black, built with double decks, and like other productions of the Short shipyards was given a fine rating; the cabins were panelled in walnut with reeded walnut pilasters and capitals exquisitely carved and decorated in gold leaf. The *Chipman,* unlike the other Short built ships, was masted, wholly rigged, and very nearly completed before the launching.

The christening and launching of this ship was a very noteworthy event; St. Stephen was alive with excitement as two thousand people gathered along the river to watch this ship take the water. The launching took place while the tide was fairly low; should the vessel not slide down the ways it would be floated by the incoming high tide.

When the vessel started to slide all of the stays on the port side fell down, the ship careened over to a thirty-degree angle toward the wharf, those on board had to hang on for fear of being thrown about as the vessel keeled over far enough to give spectators a view of everything on deck, and the ship struck the corner of the wharf in passing but was not damaged. The fully rigged ship was then towed to The Ledge on the St. Croix River where details were completed and Captain Lewis took command on the 15th day of May; he later sailed to Saint John for a cargo and the maiden voyage to Liverpool.

The ship *Chipman* was surveyed at Cardiff in 1883 and later sold to Wilhelm Wilhelmsen of Tonsberg, Norway, and was last surveyed at Dublin, Ireland, in 1893. This ship made many successful voyages to England, Ireland, Norway, and Sweden. Though given only a nine year rating the vessel was still in service after sixteen years.

The *Chipman* was 192 feet long,
36 feet breadth, 22 feet depth of hold;
1,083 tons.

Ship	*Rocklands*
	Launched in 1878
	Captain James Farr

The *Rocklands* was built by Messrs. John and Charles Short for Zachariah Chipman, Esq., and was the last ship to be built by this justly celebrated firm. It was launched from the Short Shipyards at St. Stephen on October 1, 1878; a large crowd gathered to watch the event. The ship was christened by Miss Jessie Tilley, daughter of Sir Samuel Leonard Tilley of St. John, who at one time was a strong advocate of confederation, a minister in the Canadian cabinet, and later twice a Lieutenant Governor of New Brunswick.

The *Rocklands* was built under the special survey of the Bureau of Veritus to Class 3.3.1.1., received one of the highest classifications ever given by Lloyd's of London, and was the finest and most beautiful of all the St. Croix built vessels.

The bow was finely moulded and adorned with a handsome billet head carved with elaborate scrollwork laid in gold leaf; the stern piece was also magnificently carved and gilded and was placed on the rounded stern. The quarter deck aft was raised about six feet and was known as a flush quarter deck, being the same height from rail to rail.

The three lower masts came from British Columbia by way of Cape Horn and were first landed at Boston, then reshipped to St. Stephen. The fore and main masts were about ninety feet long and about thirty-six inches in diameter at the butt end; the cost of the lower masts alone was one thousand dollars.

The cabins were finished in walnut, satinwood, ash, and the finest of white pine; the panelling and pilasters were of walnut, the capitals being exquisitely carved and lined with gold. Some of the smaller mouldings had gold leaf as well, making the cabins exceptionally beautiful.

The *Rocklands* was not fully rigged before the launching, but the lower masts, shrouds, bowsprit, and fore chains were all in place. After the launching, the vessel was towed to The Ledge on the St. Croix where the rigging was completed. There Captain Farr took command of his ship which was then registered at St. Andrews and sailed to St. John to load a cargo for the maiden voyage to Liverpool. Soon afterward the *Rocklands* joined the well-known Ring Fleet, and later was sold to J. S. De Wolf of Liverpool.

In 1881, the *St. Helena Guardian* printed part of a report by Captain Farr stressing the gallant heroism of his crew which voluntarily risked their lives while sailing around the Cape of Good Hope in the midst of a hurricane:

> In order to save the rudder, which could not have lasted 24 hours longer, I saw nothing would do but a good chain lashing, and I determined with the aid of Providence to bring the ship around the cape. My carpenter, Mark C. Cavanaugh, of St. Stephen, and third mate, James Langmaid, of St. Andrews, both natives of New Brunswick, volunteered to be hung over the stern in bowlines, to pass a chain around the stock and wedge it tightly just above the rudder blade, also to lash one strong wire around it and passing through the trunk. This double attachment made the rudder fairly firm and the means of saving it go far. It also enabled us to use the wheel a little.

The vessel was thus able to sail to St. Helena, where a new rudder was made so that the remainder of the voyage was completed in safety. The crew was honored for their heroic work in repairing and saving the old rudder at sea, as this adventure was exceedingly dangerous in heavy seas where sharks abounded.

Although most substantially built, the *Rocklands* came to a very unfortunate ending. No doubt the vessel became weakened while beating through several fiercely raging storms around Cape Horn; it foundered after another terrific storm in the English Channel on March 2, 1882. The signal letters were Q. W. H. T.

The *Rocklands* was 214 feet long,
37 feet beam, 23 feet depth of hold;
1,464 tons.

Ship

George Stetson
Built in 1880

Captains:

William S. Higgins, Bangor   Pearce, of Wiscasset

J. S. Lowell, Woolwich   Edward H. Wood, Wiscasset

The *George Stetson* was built at Bath, Maine, in 1880, especially for the San Francisco trade. It was built under supervision of the American Shipmasters' Association, classed under Special Survey, and given a twelve-year rating by Lloyd's.

The vessel was last registered at San Francisco in 1884, and P. M. Whitmore and others were given as the owners in 1885. The signal letters were J. T. S. V.

The *George Stetson* was 232 feet long, 41 feet breadth, 26 feet depth of hold; 1,845 gross tons.

51

Schooner   ## Jesse H. Freeman

Built in 1883
Captain William H. Robertson, 1883
Captain John Manson, 1893

The *Jesse H. Freeman,* a three-masted schooner, was built by Goss &
Sawyer Company at Bath, Maine, in 1883, under the special supervision
of the American Shipmasters' Association, and was given a thirteen-
year rating. The *Freeman* was one of several sailing vessels built at Bath
equipped with auxiliary engines which enabled the vessel to make port
and landings without the aid of tugboats; this schooner had two auxiliary engines of 300 horsepower each.

The vessel was of graceful design, painted black, and had a real
Down East quality, with a caboose and a finely carved billet head and
gold scrollwork on the bow.

This interesting portrait shows the schooner steaming under its
own power without the aid of tugboats or the use of sail. The vessel's
signal letters were K. B. D. W.

First owned by Standard Steam Navigation Company, in service
from Boston to Jamaica, the *Freeman* was especially designed for the
transportation of fruit. Later the vessel was purchased by the Boston
Fruit Company, and is said to be the beginning of the United Fruit
Company's Great White Fleet.

In 1885, the *Jesse H. Freeman* was sold to the San Francisco Whaling Company and rebuilt as a barkentine, remaining in their service
until 1910, at which time it was again sold as a "dude type whaler."
Finally converted into a barge, the vessel ended its days in this service.

> The *Jesse H. Freeman* was 146 feet long,
> 30 feet breadth, 17 feet depth of hold;
> 516 gross tons and 359 net tons.

Ship

Benjamin F. Packard

Built in 1883

Captains:

John Waterhouse	Zaccheus Allen, 1889-1904
J. R. Kelly — owner in 1893	D. J. Martin
C. W. Jackson	J. Allen
D. A. St. Clair	Frank H. Jaeger

The ship *Benjamin F. Packard* was built by the firm of Goss, Sawyer & Packard at Bath, Maine, in 1883, and was named for a member of the firm. This ship was the last one built by this company, and on the completion of the vessel Mr. Packard became superintendent of the New England Shipbuilding Company at Bath. Mr. Packard came from Wiscasset and started work in shipyards at Bath in 1850.

Ship *Packard* was built especially for the California trade at the cost of $250,000. The vessel was a medium class clipper type square rigger with double decks, a billet head and rounded stern; this ship was given a fifteen-year rating by the American Shipmasters' Association. The *Packard* was not a clipper ship but a Down East cargo carrier designed for speed and freight capacity, being exceptionally well built.

The *Packard* made many successful voyages to San Francisco and other North Pacific Coast ports, as well as fair passages to Honolulu, England, and Japan. For several years the *Packard* was owned and managed by Captain John R. Kelly, and for twenty years the vessel was owned by Arthur Sewall & Company of Bath.

Although sailing records of the *Packard* have always been disputed, this ship is said to have made a record passage from San Francisco to New York in 83 days; this would have been possible sailing down from San Francisco with favorable winds and a hard driving captain. This record would exceed those of the clipper ship *Flying Cloud* and the medium clipper type ship *Andrew Jackson* whose records had never been surpassed on a voyage from New York to the Pacific port by any other sailing vessel, though they have been equalled.

It was April 15, 1892, that the ship, laden with cargo, sailed from San Francisco to New York arriving on July 18th, making the passage in 94 days; this voyage is the one often said to have been made in 83 days; the dispute has never been settled, but the 94-day run is probably correct. Average passages made by the *Packard* from New York to San Francisco, usually a long, hard voyage, were 148 days; two runs were made in 130 days each, three runs were made between 150 and 160 days, and others from 163 days to 172 days, the last being the slowest on record.

Ship *Packard* met with a number of mishaps while rounding Cape Horn, but none were of a very serious nature.

In February of 1902, Captain Zaccheus Allen encountered the roughest weather of his career while sailing the *Packard* from British Columbia to San Francisco; throughout the whole run, heavy gales were roaring and the ship was flooded most of the time.

In 1908, the *Packard* was sold by A. Sewall & Company to the Northwestern Fisheries Company of Seattle, and sailed to Alaska in the salmon fishing fleet for many years after.

The vessel was again sold in 1924 to a Pacific coast lumber company which loaded the *Packard* with lumber and towed the vessel through the Panama Canal to New York. On the arrival in New York Harbor, efforts were made to preserve the vessel as a Marine Museum, for this was one of the last of the typical Down East ships and one of the most substantially built ones ever known, the vessel having proved to be superior to the clipper ships in every way, with moderately fast sailing records and good cargo capacity. However, there was not enough interest shown in preserving the *Packard* so the vessel was towed back to the Pacific coast where it was purchased by Mr. Theodore Roosevelt Pell, the well-known yachtsman; further efforts were made to transform the ship into a Maritime Museum, but these also failed. Later the vessel was loaned for a Junior Naval Reserve Training Ship. Finally the *Packard* was sold at Manhasset Bay, Long Island, to a Boston antique dealer with its masts, spars, and rigging all complete; the vessel was fully restored and used as a museum where ship models were made and exhibited by the Ship Model Makers Club. Once again the *Packard* changed owners, and in 1930 was tied up at an amusement park pier known as Playland at Rye, New York. After several years of service here, the vessel was condemned, towed out to sea, and sunk. Captain Frank Jaeger of Rockport, Maine, the ship's last captain, rescued the beautifully carved billet head and the engraved bronze capstan cap which are now in his marine collection; a table from this vessel may also be seen in the Marine Historical Collection at Mystic, Connecticut.

Captain Jaeger was the last man to step off the ship before it sank beneath the wave. The signal letters of the *Packard* were K. B. V. T., and the vessel was manned by a crew of fifteen. Though this ship had been given only a fifteen-year rating it was in use for over forty-seven years; this was one of the last and most durable of Maine wooden built ships.

The *Benjamin F. Packard* was 244 feet long,
43 feet breadth, 18 feet depth of hold;
2,156 gross tons and 2,013 net tons.

Steam barkentine   *Morning Star*
Built in 1884
Captain Bray
Captain J. Turner

The *Morning Star* was built for the American Missionary Society by the New England Shipbuilding Company at Bath, Maine. It was launched on August 6, 1884, and sailed from Boston on November 5, 1884, with a crew of forty-three.

The vessel was barkentine rigged, with an auxiliary steam engine of one hundred horsepower. It was designed with a female figurehead pointing her right hand and holding the Bible in the other.

The *Morning Star* was sold at San Francisco in 1907 and renamed the *Herman*. Still later, it was sold to foreign interests.

The *Morning Star* was 131 feet long, 29½ feet in breadth, 12 feet in depth; 410 gross tons and 229 net tons.

Ship   *Frederick Billings*

Built in 1885

Captains:

   Isaac W. Sherman, Camden   "Bert" Williams, Thomaston
   W. H. Freeman   Everett Staples
   George T. Harkness

Mate: Edward Meady of Yarmouth, Maine

The *Frederick Billings* was launched from the shipyards of Carleton, Norwood & Company at Rockport, Maine, in August, 1885. Pascal & Company were the master builders. This large vessel followed the ship *Ocean King* as the second four-masted ship to be built in this country after the *Great Republic,* and is said to have been one of the strongest vessels ever constructed of wood up to that time. It was given a fifteen-year rating, and the signal letters K. D. C. T. Camden and Rockport, Maine, were well-known for the hardy quality of their vessels, and everything for the equipment of these ocean going craft was produced in both towns.

Built especially for the New York-California trade, the *Frederick Billings* was advertised to load at New York for San Francisco on its maiden voyage. However, a better charter for a cargo of case oil for Japan was arranged, so that the vessel sailed southeastward for Japan and crossed to San Francisco, in continuation of this first voyage, arriving in June, 1886. The vessel then sailed around Cape Horn to Havre with a cargo of wheat, making the passage in 112 days.

Captain Isaac W. Sherman of Camden, Maine, was the first master and was continuously in command, except for one passage, until 1890, when he sold his interest and retired from the sea. He had started seafaring as a boy in one of his father's vessels, signing on as a cook. He became captain of the coasting schooner *Brilliant* and from 1856 on was chiefly in the East India trade. Captain Sherman was master of the well-known ship *Highlander,* which was attacked and burned by the Confederate warship *Alabama* in 1863; he was also captain of the ships *Art Union, Bennington, Success, Joseph Clark,* and *Reaper.* He had been captain of the *Reaper* for several years before taking command of the *Frederick Billings.* He was in command of the vessel on a particularly long passage to San Francisco in 1889, which took 145 days. Captain Sherman later said that it was the most trying passage he had ever made. The weather was very bad, with strong winds continuing for 55 days.

During Captain Sherman's entire career he never lost a vessel, never had a protest for damage, and never had to put into port for supplies. In 1888, he achieved fame in a political way, being elected a State Senator from Knox County, Maine, polling some 500 more votes than his opponent.

In 1890, the celebrated Captain Herbert H. Williams, former master of the ship *St. Paul* bought shares in the *Frederick Billings* while the vessel was at Liverpool, and became captain. His second passage to San Francisco was a most difficult one. Sailing from New York on October 31, 1891, the vessel encountered variable winds until November 6th. Orders had been given to clew up the royals, and three men were on the fore royal yard and three on the main royal, when a bad squall struck. The starboard martingale backstay gave way, causing an immediate breaking off of the jibboom at the cap and of the fore- and main-topmasts at the eyes of the rigging. They all came down with a thundering crash. One of the men aloft managed to catch hold of some rigging and escaped with a few bruises. The other five were never seen again, as the vessel was unmanageable in a heavy pounding sea and nothing could be done to save them. After the squall had passed away the wreckage was cut off, and Captain Williams continued the voyage although under very trying circumstances. He was fortunate in having Edward Meady as his Chief Mate.

One of the first things Captain Williams had done on taking command of the *Billings* was to have a fine engine installed for hoisting work. This proved fortuitous, otherwise the vessel would have been obliged to put into some port for repairs. By working day and night, they made over a main-topmast; put it in place just one week after the squall. Two days later a main-topgallant mast was sent up, and work was started on a fore-topmast. Later the vessel set fore- and main-skysails and looked smartly, as if nothing had ever happened; new spars had been made of the spare material.

Thirty-three days out the vessel had crossed the line, but fell to leeward off Cape St. Rogue and lost a week drifting around. During the 17 days it took to round Cape Horn a seaman was killed by falling from aloft to the deck. This was the last misfortune of the passage.

The *Billings* arrived in port in first-class condition, all repairs having been made at sea. On arrival Captain Williams was arrested for alleged cruelty to his seamen, but the charges were unceremoniously dismissed. Later he was honored for his seamanship and ability in handling the dismasted vessel and presented with a cheque for a substantial sum by the Board of Underwriters.

On the last arrival of the *Billings* at San Francisco from New York, the vessel was chartered for a shipment of nitrate from the West Coast to Hampton Roads. By July 29, 1893, the vessel had taken aboard 3,800 tons in eight working days, the fastest loading of any ship known up to that date, and was scheduled to sail the following morning. At nine o'clock in the evening, while Captain Williams was in his cabin writing up his accounts, the watchman on deck reported a fire on board. Almost immediately a series of terrific explosions occurred, all the decks and sides of the vessel suddenly burst upward and outward in every direction. Twenty minutes after the alarm had been given, there was nothing left of the vessel but a mass of floating wreckage. Though some of the crew had been obliged to jump overboard, all hands were saved, mostly by boats from nearby vessels.

A thorough investigation failed to establish the truth of reports that the crew were responsible for the destruction of the ship. It was claimed that they had received very harsh treatment on the last passage and that many of the seamen had been prevented from deserting only by the alertness of the boatswain.

Known as Captain "Bert", Captain Williams was a native of Thomaston, Maine, succeeding his partner, Captain Thomas C. Williams, as master of the *St. Paul* in 1882. After leaving the *Billings* he became master of a whale ship sailing from San Francisco, and later commander of the steamer *Oregonian*. The *Oregonian* belonged to the American-Hawaiian Steamship Company, and Captain Williams became that company's first superintendent.

Chief Mate Edward Meady of Yarmouth, Maine, was the last officer to leave the burning ship. After the death of Captain W. H. Freeman, who had been temporarily relieving Captain Williams, Chief Mate Meady had once navigated the *Billings* from San Francisco to New York. His wife was the only woman aboard the ship, and she acted as stewardess. He was a thoroughly competent seaman.

Though the *Billings* made many good passages, it was not considered one of the so-called fast Down Easters. Other voyages were made in the following times: Cardiff to San Francisco in 126 days; San Francisco to Liverpool in 122 days; San Francisco to Havre in 117 days; San Francisco to Liverpool in 132 days; New York to San Francisco in 135 days; San Francisco to Havre in 115 days; and New York to San Francisco in 135 days.

The *Frederick Billings* was 278 feet long, 44 feet breadth, 29 feet depth of hold; 2,497 gross tons and 4,100 net tons.

Barque   *Annie C. Maguire*

Built in 1853
Captain Rowland T. Delano, 1879
Captain Thomas O'Neil

The Portland Head Lighthouse was ordered built by President George Washington and was approved by Alexander Hamilton while he was Secretary of the Treasury. Congress appropriated the funds for its completion, and this famous beacon was first lighted on January 10, 1791.

This lighthouse and the Portsmouth Harbor Head Light, built in 1789, were the only beacons serving the northern New England coast for many years. Later the Portland light was lowered and its power reduced; mariners complained so much that the original height of the beacon was restored, and a more modern lantern and lens installed. Now its brilliant flash may be seen far away at sea, and a fog horn sounds at regular intervals during storms and foggy weather.

On December 24, 1886, a wild and turbulent sea tossed the *Annie C. Maguire* literally into the lap of Portland Head Light. She was on the last leg of a long voyage from Buenos Aires to Quebec when a raging blizzard struck, and Captain O'Neil chose to run for the safety of Portland Harbor so that his wife and young son, together with the fifteen men comprising the crew, might enjoy the Christmas holidays ashore. Terrified observers along shore could plainly see his vessel was sailing right for certain doom on the jagged rocks which face the ocean just below the Head Light tower. The lighthouse keeper, Joshua Strout, with his son, Joseph, did everything possible to signal the captain, but the blizzard was too dense. They quickly set about rigging a breeches buoy, and as the *Annie C. Maguire* piled high onto the rocks, a two-inch rope was thrown out from shore to the vessel and made fast around the crosstrees. The captain and his family and all the crew were then hauled to safety in a boatswain's chair. This gallant rescue was characteristic of the hardy resourcefulness of the lighthouse service.

The barque *Annie C. Maguire* of Buenos Aires was formerly the celebrated clipper ship *Golden State* of New York. The *Golden State* was owned by the well-known A. A. Low & Brother, built at New York in 1853, rebuilt in 1869, and again rebuilt in 1872.

The *Annie C. Maguire* was 186 feet long, 40 feet breadth, 21 feet depth of hold; 944 tons.

65

Schooner   *Governor Ames*

Launched in 1888
Captain C. A. Davis
Captain King

The *Governor Ames* was the first five-masted schooner to be built on the Atlantic Coast, and was named for a former governor of Massachusetts, Oliver Ames, who was in office from 1886 to 1888.

This vessel was built at Waldoboro, Maine, and the rare photograph shows the *Ames* just before the launching on December 1, 1888, near the head tide of the Medomak River.

The *Governor Ames* was owned in 1893 by C. A. Davis of Fall River, Massachusetts; it was registered at New York in 1900, and later at Providence, Rhode Island, in 1908. The signal letters were K. G. C. T. This schooner was last surveyed at San Francisco, and was stranded on the Pacific Coast in 1910.

The *Governor Ames* was 245 feet long, 49 feet breadth, 21 feet depth of hold; 1778 gross tons, 1690 net tons.

Ship

Henry B. Hyde

Built in 1884

Captains:

Phineas Pendleton, 3rd
John G. Pendleton
James P. Butman
Joshua B. Nichols

Theodore P. Colcord
D. A. Scribner
William McLeod
L. T. Amesbury

The *Henry B. Hyde* was a famous ship, considered one of the finest Down Easters ever built by the master builder John McDonald in the Bath shipyard of Benjamin Flint & Company, of New York. It was named after the president of the Equitable Life Insurance Company.

The vessel had the distinction of being the largest ship built in Maine up to the time of launching in November, 1884, and was constructed in the strongest possible manner and of the best materials obtainable. The hull was cross-braced with iron straps 45 feet long, 5 inches wide and 5/6 of an inch thick. The yellow-pine planking was 5 inches thick and the frame was of heavy white oak. More than 200 tons of iron were used in the construction, also 4425 sheets of copper, as the *Hyde* was metaled on the stocks. It was given a fifteen-year rating; its signal letters were K. C. S. V.

The yards on the fore- and mainmasts were of the same dimensions, and in length were as follows: lowers, 90 feet; lower topsails, 82 feet; uppers, 74 feet; topgallants, 61 feet; royals, 50 feet; and skysail yards, 40 feet. The vessel had wire rigging and cost upwards of $125,000. The *Hyde* was undoubtedly one of the finest wooden ships ever built in this or any other country.

On the ship's arrival at New York, on December 1, 1884, 26 days after it had left the ways in Bath, the *Shipping List* said:

The *Henry B. Hyde* is as fine a specimen of marine architecture as ever entered this or any other port, and as speed has not entirely been overlooked in the make-up of her model, it is expected that she will make good time on her run out of the Golden Gate.

The vessel was built for the San Francisco trade, and practically its whole sea life was spent therein. Of the sixteen completed round voyages, thirteen outward runs were made from New York, two from Baltimore, and the other from Norfolk to Honolulu. One return was with nitrate from Caleta Buena; seven were with grain to Liverpool; four were to New York direct; and the other four from Honolulu to New York.

The *Hyde* left New York on its maiden voyage on February 24, 1885, with a crew of three mates, a boatswain, carpenter, sailmaker, cook, steward, cabin boy and twenty-four men before the mast. The passage to San Francisco took 123 days, during which fore- and main-topgallant masts were carried away in a heavy squall 16 days out, though the *Hyde* still managed to cross the Line on the 23rd day at sea. It encountered much light weather in the North Pacific, and was 31 days from the equator to port. On the return voyage from San Francisco to Liverpool, the ship took 96 days.

Between 1890 and 1893, the *Hyde* made four passages from New York to San Francisco in 108, 108, 105 and 112 days. The average of all outward passages to the Golden Gate was 124 days, 153 days being the longest. On the latter occasion, which was in 1900, Captain McLeod reported having nothing but adverse winds throughout, with a long spell of very bad weather off Cape Horn.

The average of the *Hyde's* seven passages from San Francisco to the United Kingdom was 107 days; 96 days was the fastest, and 114 days the slowest. The four runs to New York were made in 88, 94, 135 and 110 days respectively.

The 88-day passage from San Francisco to New York was made in 1888 while Captain John G. Pendleton was in command, relieving his nephew, Phineas Pendleton. Captain Selwyn McGilvery of Searsport, formerly master of the ship *David Brown* was chief mate. The ship had a full cargo of refined sugar, 60,791 bags. Moderate to light winds were experienced in the Pacific, and Cape Horn was not rounded until the 50th day out. Thereafter, however, remarkably fast time was made, the ship being only 19 days from the Cape to the Line and 19 days thence to port.

Mr. Amos D. Carver, now of Baker, Carver & Morrill of New York, whose father, Captain George A. Carver, was then a member of that firm, distinctly recalls the arrival of the ship and recounts the following incident:

When the *Henry B. Hyde* was reported to my father as being off the Hook in tow, the number of days she was out were checked up and found to be 87. My father said the report must be in error. Later, Captain Pendleton came walking into the office and extended his hand with the inquiry, "Well, George, how are you? Any letters from home for me?" "No, John," was the reply. "We were not looking for your arrival for 3 weeks. I'll say, John, you sure made a fine run." "Fair, George, only fair," was the response. "I'd have broken the record if we hadn't been becalmed ten days near the Pacific equator."

In 1889, this ship made a passage from San Francisco to Honolulu in 9 days and 4½ hours; four passages from the Hawaiian Islands to New York were made in 100, 109, 104, and 133 days. A passage from Caleta Buena to New York was made in 80 days in spite of losing jib-booms, fore- and main-topgallant masts and some yards in a sudden squall 10 days out. On a 96-day passage from San Francisco to Liverpool, favorable weather was encountered and the ship arrived off Lymas after 95 days and 6 hours; from Liverpool the *Hyde* crossed to New York in 22 days and had logged some 35,000 miles in 241 sailing days, carrying 8,800 tons of cargo, since first leaving New York.

The *Henry B. Hyde* met with a number of mishaps during the course of its voyages, some of which came near being very serious. On several occasions important spars and sails were carried away, and in 1886 the ship was badly damaged by a collision in San Francisco Bay. While being towed by a tug the vessel got foul of the ship *Parker M. Whitmore,* and both vessels drifted down on the whaling bark *Northern Light;* all three were damaged before being separated.

A momentous passage made by the *Hyde* from New York to San Francisco was reported by Captain Scribner on his arrival in December, 1897. It appeared that among his crew there wasn't a single sailor; all were Bowery pugilists and other rough characters, and each and every one was at least semi-mutinous during the whole run. Captain and officers were at the mercy of the mob without having any recourse; they were merely allowed to navigate the ship while the crew did as they pleased.

In October, 1899, the *Henry B. Hyde* was sold with the rest of the large fleet of sailing ships belonging to Benjamin Flint & Company to the California Shipping Company of San Francisco, and they remained owners until it was lost.

On the voyage from Norfolk to Honolulu, in 1899-1900, the coal cargo of the *Hyde* was discovered to be on fire, and the ship was steered for Valparaiso where it was all discharged. After a delay of some seven weeks the voyage was resumed with about 1,700 tons which had been reloaded, and Honolulu was made after a passage of 38 days from the Chilean port.

In 1902, the *Hyde* had another experience with fire in its cargo. It had left Baltimore on May 18th for San Francisco, and when in the vicinity of Cape Horn the coal cargo was found to be badly heated. Captain McLeod decided it wisest to run for Cape Town and anchored in Table Bay on August 19th. There, some 600 tons were discharged and the voyage resumed; the ship arrived in San Francisco on December 25th, having been 221 days out from Baltimore and 82 days from Cape Town. This round voyage, the last made by the *Henry B. Hyde,* was completed on the return run from San Francisco to New York in 110 days.

At New York the command of the *Hyde* was given to Captain Pearson, formerly second officer of the Pacific Mail Steamer *City of Peking,* and left in tow for Baltimore to load for San Francisco. On February 19, 1904, the ship broke adrift from its tug during a heavy gale and was washed ashore at Dam Neck Life Saving Station, some ten miles south of Cape Henry. Wrecking steamers were unable to render assistance, but their sailors unloaded the ship's stores and the crew were safely landed. The vessel soon became badly sanded, and while the storm continued, it was sold as it lay. Later the ship was floated, but another bad storm came up and it was again driven ashore. During the night of October 4th the *Henry B. Hyde* broke in two. More than a year afterward it was reported that the wreck was to be blown up in an effort to recover the masts.

Captain Phineas Pendleton, 3rd, was born in Searsport in 1832; his parents were Captain Phineas, 2nd, and wealthy Carver Pendleton. When quite young he succeeded his father as master of the barques *Henry Buck* and *Phineas Pendleton,* and in 1864 was given command of the new ship *David Brown.* Later he was master of the ships Bosphorus, *R. B. Fuller, Nancy Pendleton, St. Nicholas, Manuel Llaguna, Elizabeth* and *Henry B. Hyde,* being appointed to the last three ships before they were launched. On relinquishing command of the *Hyde* in 1897, he retired from the sea for about five years, and ran a fruit ranch in the Santa Clara Valley in California. He then returned east and spent most of his time at his home in Searsport. During the winter he stayed with a daughter living in Worcester, Massachusetts, and passed on there in April, 1909, but was buried in his home town. The Captain was one of the most able and successful early shipmasters.

Captain William J. McLeod, who made two voyages in the *Henry B. Hyde* toward the end of his career, was a native of Nova Scotia and sailed in vessels owned there for many years. After arriving on the Pacific Coast he took command of the *Rufus E. Wood* for a time, and on relinquishing the captaincy of the *Hyde,* had the steel four-masted bark *John Ena.* He passed on in San Francisco in 1924.

> The *Henry B. Hyde* was 267 feet length of keel,
> 290 feet over-all length,
> 45 feet beam, 29 feet depth of hold;
> 2,583 gross tons and 2,462 net tons.

72

Schooner

Jonathan Bourne

Built in 1883
Captain W. C. Thompson
Captain Kelly

The *Jonathan Bourne* was the first four-masted schooner to be built by Holly M. Bean, at Camden, Maine, and was the eighth schooner of this type to be built in the United States. It was given a thirteen-year rating and the signal letters K. B. S. H.

The *King Philip* and the *Mount Hope* were the second and third four-masted vessels built at Camden. Camden was noted for its fine vessels and the industrial capacity to furnish complete nautical equipment for them; everything necessary for a ship or schooner was made right in the town. Local men usually commanded these vessels after they were completed.

The *Jonathan Bourne* was first registered at Newport, Rhode Island, and later at Harwich, Massachusetts; Osmyn Berry & Company were the owners at that time.

The *Jonathan Bourne* was 172 feet long, 35 feet breadth, 12 feet depth of hold; 708 gross tons and 673 net tons.

Shipentine *Shenandoah*

Launched in 1890

Captains:

James Murphy   E. A. Watts
William H. Dumphy   J. Wilder Murphy
William H. Starky   O. E. Chapman

The *Shenandoah,* sometimes called a four-masted barque, was the fourth four-masted square rigger and second largest wooden sailing vessel in capacity ever constructed in this country. It was built by Arthur Sewall & Company, Bath, Maine, at a cost of $175,000. The frame of the vessel was moulded by Charles Short of St. Stephen, New Brunswick, at Bishop's Crossing, Quebec, and was launched in November, 1890; about 8,000 people gathered to watch the vessel slide down the ways.

This vessel, like many other Maine built ships, was a combination of both old and new ideas. Economic and technical factors were of the utmost importance in the building of these ships for the Cape Horn-San Francisco trade, with the hope of competing with the fast steamships at that time. The *Shenandoah,* designed with a square stern, was one of the real so-called Down Easters which meant that the ship was exceptionally well built, as smart as a clipper ship, and could hold a large cargo. Only the *Great Republic, Three Brothers,* and *Frederick Billings* could compare to the *Shenandoah* in size.

From 1860 to 1900, most of the important wooden ships and sailing vessels were built in Maine and New Brunswick, and the Down Easters proved to be the finest development of all the wooden sailing vessels. They were considered superior to the over-dramatized and romantic clipper, whose life span was about thirteen years.

At the time of its building many feared a wooden vessel of such great length would be unsteady in heavy seas. However, the *Shenandoah* was built in the strongest possible manner, with four extra frames used in the midship section. Eight hundred tons of hard wood were used in building the frame, and one half million feet in the planking, ceilings, and other parts of the vessel. It was sheathed to 25 feet with over 5,000 sheets of metal, using several thousand pounds of nails.

The spars of the three forward masts of the ship were nearly identical in size, the lower masts being 89 feet long and 38 inches in diameter. The top masts were 56 feet long, the topgallant, royal and skysail masts 69 feet. The lower topsail yards were 84 feet; upper top-gallants 66; royals 56; and skysail yards 46 feet. The spanker or jigger mast was 96 feet in height, 26 inches in diameter, and its top mast 82 feet in height.

The steel spike bowsprit was 43 feet outboard and 30 inches in diameter. The spread of canvas was 11,000 yards. It was not as heavily sparred and rigged as a medium clipper. It had wooden anchor stocks, rope steering tackles, modern side light towers, steam wind-lass, steam winch, and rigging screws. One of the anchors weighed 6,800 pounds and the other 6,400 pounds. When first built it was painted light gray, but later changed to black to cover up bilge water stains, tar splotches, and rust and iron stains. It was given a fifteen-year rating by the American Shipmasters' Association.

The vessel proved to be seaworthy in all respects. It handled well and steered easily in all weather. Though built especially for the Cape Horn-San Francisco trade, it made voyages to Liverpool and Havre, making one record sailing from Havre to New York in 32 days.

The *Shenandoah* was considered by English mariners to be the fastest sailing ship ever to sail under the Stars and Stripes. There were many reasons why British interest thought this vessel the best and fastest wooden ship owned by an American company, among them the fact that the ship always sailed with a cargo, the owners never had to worry about a charter, the vessel never laid in port, and was known as one of the best cargo ships built on the Atlantic coast.

The crew, as on nearly all of the Down Easters, consisted of captain, three mates, a carpenter, boatswain, donkey man, steward, cook, cabin boy, apprentices, and about twenty-five able-bodied seamen. Its first captain was Captain James Murphy, and others were Captain William H. Dumphy, Captain William H. Starky, Captain E. A. Watts, Captain J. Wilder Murphy (the son of the first Captain), and Captain O. I. Chapman.

The *Shenandoah* had many mishaps, but a successful and eventful career. It came within two days of equalling a clipper ship run from New York to San Francisco, once racing the *Tam O' Shanter* on this run. The *Shenandoah* arrived off the bar several days in advance but was delayed by a fogbank approaching the Golden Gate. When the fog lifted both vessels entered port on the same day; *Tam O' Shanter* managed to get a towboat and thus was considered to have reached port first.

An interesting episode occurred during a passage from San Francisco to Liverpool when Captain Murphy was given a warning by the captain of a British tramp steamer that Spanish torpedo boats were on the lookout for his famous vessel. Later another British captain also warned him of waiting torpedo boats and towed the *Shenandoah* up the coast until within the three-mile limit, at which time a Liverpool tug was picked up. The owners then instructed Captain Murphy to insure the vessel against war risks for a safe passage from Liverpool to Baltimore. Instead of insuring the vessel, the Captain placed two four-inch guns on his vessel, one at the bow and one at the stern. Four days out, under full sail, the *Shenandoah* encountered a Spanish gunboat which fired a shot across the bow. It not only held its course, but fired two rounds at the gunboat which soon disappeared.

Another interesting incident happened during one of the voyages of the famous ship *Cutty Sark* to Sydney, Australia, when her Captain spotted a big four-masted vessel sailing under lower topsail and foresail. The *Cutty Sark,* having all sail set to royals, signalled the shipentine, but received no reply. It was getting dark, the glass was falling rapidly, and there were signs of a blow; when the captain of the shipentine noted the *Cutty Sark* canvas he began to hoist sail rapidly and had set the main royal just as darkness came. Captain Woodget of the *Cutty Sark* noted the color and rigging of the shipentine in his log, describing it undoubtedly as the *Shenandoah,* with the notation that the captain evidently did not want to be talked about. For some reason many American vessels did not answer when signalled, but the big *Shenandoah* later signalled the *Cutty Sark* when they passed off Cape Horn.

Unfortunately this vessel, like many other wooden ships, ended its days as a coal barge, and finally was rammed and sunk by a steamship near Fire Island, New York. Eventually the submerged hulk was blown up by the United States Coast Guard.

The *Shenandoah* was 299 feet long,
49 feet breadth, 29 feet depth of hold;
3,407 gross tons and 3,258 net tons.

George W. Wells
Built in 1900
Captain A. L. Crowley

The *George W. Wells* was the first six-masted schooner of its kind to be built on the Atlantic Coast. Designed by B. J. Wardwell and built at the shipyards of Holly M. Bean, Camden, Maine, it is said to have cost $90,000. This schooner made 15 knots an hour in a good breeze, and could carry 5,000 tons of coal, the largest cargo known for any wooden ship at that time; it was given a fifteen-year rating, and the signal letters were K. Q. G. L.

The schooner was named for George W. Wells, of Southbridge, Massachusetts, and was christened by Miss Mary Wells on August 4, 1900. Miss Wells threw a large bunch of white roses at the bow and released a flock of white pigeons as the vessel slid down the ways. The launching ceremonies were concluded with a dance at the Camden Opera House given by the young ladies of the town, and attended by the officers of the visiting battleships *Indiana* and *Kearsarge*. It was one of the most exciting events in the history of this seaport town.

The photograph at left shows the big schooner riding at anchor in Camden Harbor as the final rigging was being completed. The *Wells* carried a crew of thirteen men.

The schooner *Eleanor Percy,* the second six-masted schooner to be built on the Atlantic Coast, was in collision with the *George W. Wells* on her maiden voyage off Cape Cod on July 9, 1901. Both vessels were badly damaged, but reconditioned and again placed in service.

The *George W. Wells* was wrecked in a hurricane on the North Carolina coast in 1913, and was a complete loss to the owners. There were only ten six-masted schooners ever built in this country.

> The *George W. Wells* was 319 feet long, 48 feet breadth, 23 feet depth of hold; 2,970 gross tons, and 2,743 net tons.

Barkentine   *Eleanor M. Williams*

Built in 1890
Captain Daniel E. Corbett

The *Eleanor M. Williams* was built by John Shaw, the master builder of Machias, Maine. There were a number of shareholders in this vessel, some of whom were: John Shaw, Charles Inglee, H. E. Saunders, Daniel E. Corbett, Annie T. Corbett, Mary A. Thompson, G. Harris Foster, William C. Holway, Charles J. McLaughlin of Machias, Charles H. Welch, Zemro H. Thompson of Machiasport, Hattie P. Wilder of Cutler, Henry P. Dewey of Portland, James E. Brett, Belcher T. Thurlow, Hattie P. Thurlow, Tristram T. Corbett, David J. Taft, John T. Langhill, Alexander O. Williams, Willardson and Johnson, Sarah Burgess and Oliver O. Terrill of New York City.

Designed and built with a billet head and rounded stern, this barkentine was used principally for the transportation of lumber; she was given a thirteen-year rating, and was still in service in 1902. The signal letters were K. H. R. C.

The *Eleanor M. Williams* was an ill-fated ship. Originally built for the Brazil coffee trade, during her first voyage she laid in a Brazilian port for almost nine months waiting for a return shipment of coffee. The demurrage charges came to one-half her value and on her return she had to be replanked. In those days Mr. Shaw did not copper his ships until they had earned enough money for the coppering job.

On a subsequent trip the stern was ripped off in a collision with a steamer, and later a heavy storm dismasted her.

From 1847 to 1890 John Shaw built a total of 56 vessels, representing a complete estimate of 14,575 tons. In 1890, he built the two-masted schooner, *Regina,* his last creation, which was eventually purchased by Booth Tarkington and became a long-familiar sight at her mooring in the Kennebunk River at Kennebunkport, Maine, where Mr. Tarkington used her as a studio-workshop.

> The *Eleanor M. Williams* was 159 feet long,
> 32 feet breadth, 18 feet depth of hold;
> 718 gross tons, 681 net tons.

81

Schooner   # Dorothy Palmer
Built in 1903
Captain J. C. Harding

As schooners were the last to survive the age of steam, the distinguished Palmer Fleet is well worth mentioning, with this splendid photograph of the *Dorothy Palmer,* considered by many the most beautiful of all.

Mr. William F. Palmer, an educator and instructor at Bristol Academy, Taunton, Massachusetts, became interested in ships and naval architecture. The coal schooners at Taunton became his special interest, and he later designed thirteen of a fleet of fifteen vessels built by New York and Massachusetts investors. All but one of these, the *Jane Palmer,* were built in Maine.

Other schooners of this famous fleet were the *Marie Palmer, Maude Palmer, Davis Palmer, Fannie Palmer II,* and *Fuller Palmer,* all built at Bath, Maine, and the *Harwood Palmer,* built at Waldoboro, Maine.

The fleet was later taken over by the well-known J. S. Winslow & Company, of Portland, Maine.

The *Dorothy Palmer* was built at Waldoboro in 1903 by George L. Welt and registered at Boston, Massachusetts. Her crew numbered twelve men and her signal letters were K. S. L. V.

The *Dorothy Palmer* was 294 feet long, 46 feet breadth and 22 feet depth of hold; 2,872 gross tons and 2,315 net tons.

Schooner   *Wyoming*
                  Built in 1909
                  Captain Angus McLeod

_____

The *Wyoming* was the largest and the last of the six-masted schooners to be built on the Atlantic coast, and was so named as a result of Western interest in New England shipping, especially in the coal schooners. The best-known six-masted schooners on the New England coast were the *George W. Wells,* built at Camden, Maine, the *Eleanor A. Percy,* built at Bath, Maine, and the *Wyoming,* which was built by Percy & Small Company at Bath, Maine, in 1909, at a reputed cost of $185,000.00.

This schooner was the largest wooden sailing vessel ever to be built, exceeding all others in length, even including the famous Donald McKay clipper *Great Republic.* The *Wyoming* was considered successful and easy to handle with a crew of twelve men; the signal letters were L. B. H. G.

Eastern Maine shipyards continued to build schooners until about 1919, though most of the schooner fleets were sold to Canadian interests in 1917. This splendid photograph shows the vessel under full sail.

The billet head of the *Wyoming* may still be seen at Nantucket Island; it was salvaged after the schooner was wrecked near Pollock Rip in March, 1924.

> The *Wyoming* was 329 feet long,
> 50 feet breadth, 30 feet depth of hold;
> 3,730 gross tons and 3,290 net tons.

Schooner   *Winfield S. Schuster*
Built in 1904
Captain William G. Crocker

After the decline of the so-called Golden Age of Sail, which included principally the great clipper ships, Maine shipbuilders continued with the construction of wooden sailing ships and schooners that long outlived all of the clipper ships.

The *Winfield S. Schuster* was one of the last four-masted schooners to be built at Rockport, Maine. This vessel, designed with a billet head and rounded stern, was built by Chester Pascal, the master builder for Carleton, Norwood & Company at that time. Camden and Rockport schooners were well known by shipping merchants for many years. This vessel was owned later by J. B. Crocker and others.

On November 6, 1911, this schooner foundered off the Florida coast after a heavy storm; the crew of nine men were saved; the signal letters were K. S. V. N. This splendid photograph shows the vessel at anchor in Rockport Harbor immediately after the launching.

The *Winfield S. Schuster* was 218 feet long,
42 feet breadth, 20 feet depth of hold;
1,481 gross tons and 1,220 net tons.

CHARLES SHORT
1826-1895

Way Down East sailing vessels won international recognition on every ocean when Sail ruled the sea.

Charles Short, of the celebrated firm of J. & C. Short, was ranked with the foremost ship designers and builders of his time; his name was well known and remembered for many years wherever wooden sailing vessels navigated or dropped anchor. He made many working models, the moulds of which were used for his larger ships; this was considered a great art and science at that time.

Charles Short of Chamcook, New Brunswick, started his career in the remote village of Digdeguash in Charlotte County near Passamaquoddy Bay, building the ship *Homeward Bound* at a very early age. He became a master builder and constructed many vessels at St. Andrews, New Brunswick, before 1861, including the ships *Black Swan, Lady Milton,* and *Laura.* The launching of the *Black Swan* was entertainingly recorded, as follows:

There was a legend of Saint Andrews, in shipbuilding days, that a "witch" was gathering scraps for firewood in the yard when the *Black Swan* was building. Upon being asked to leave the yard by one of the owners she is said to have cursed the *Black Swan,* vowing that when it was completed the vessel would not move down the ways even with the greatest effort.

When the vessel was ready for the launching it would not move; so the builders had to hunt up the old witch and pay her the sum of twenty dollars to attend the launching, remove the curse in person which she did and at last the vessel slid gracefully down the ways. The *Black Swan* was one of Charles Short's early beautiful ships.

In 1861, Charles Short became associated with his brothers at St. Stephen, New Brunswick, and opened shipyards with marine railways

ST. CROIX ISLAND

From the Authors' Collection

there and at Calais, Maine, directly across the St. Croix River. Some of their vessels bore the highest rating ever given by Lloyd's of London.

The six brothers of the Short family were all very able, highly skilled and talented shipwrights. John and Charles Short, for whom the firm was named, were exceptionally talented designers, and possessed great executive ability; the other brothers being highly skilled, were able to turn from one job to another with admirable versatility. Their workmanship produced some of the finest wooden vessels built by the hands of man, including the later schooners; their achievements are likely to be underestimated rather than overestimated as they built every vessel with the very finest quality and selection of woods; each ship was beautifully designed.

One, Cornelius Short, was superintendent of all the shipyards and in charge of all ironwork fixtures made by another brother, Thomas P. Short, at their own iron works.

The iron fitments were the capstans, anchors, hawse holes, chains, windlasses, iron rings that were placed around the masts, jackstays, deadeyes, binnacles, ringbolts, bitts, cleats, steering wheel supports, the pintle straps that held the rudder attached to the stern, the trusses that held the yards in place against the mast which could let them rest at a forty-five degree angle when a ship was in dock or which could let them be turned sidewise while a full sail was unfurled, filled with wind, and steadily braced.

The Shorts were also experienced as sparmakers, sailmakers, riggers, and woodcarvers. They carved the handsome figureheads, billet heads, gingerbread scrollwork, quarterboards, and the many handsome stern boards.

Many other shipwrights were employed at their yards as well, including David McRoberts of St. Andrews, N. B. Mr. McRoberts was in charge of all deck work on the vessels and the building of the deck houses, hatchways, skylights, railings and mouldings. Mr. McRoberts was associated with Mr. Charles Short for more than thirty years and there was never an unpleasant word between them.

There were a few ropewalks in the region but it is said that some rope was shipped from St. John and some from Hingham, Massachusetts; it is possible that cordage may have been sent from Plymouth to a ship chandler at the International Community as all materials used there were first rate. Every known fitment was supplied from the Short Shipyards or from The Ledge on the St. Croix River where the vessels were rigged. Many times the crew of their vessels, from

91

captain to cabin boy, were recruited from the boarding houses at The Ledge as well.

The locations of the old shipyards of the St. Croix region at Digdeguash, Brandy Cove, Lower Bay St. Andrews, Oak Bay, St. Stephen, Calais, the wharf at The Ledge, the yards below the city of Calais, and other locations of their shipyards are almost impossible to find at the present time, as all are overgrown with trees and shrubs. A shipyard at Lower Bay Saint Andrews was near the McRoberts' residence from which one formerly had a fine view and could watch all the varied activities of shipbuilding from laying of the keel to fitting out and rigging the completed vessel. A shipyard at St. Stephen was located near the Charles Short house on Prince William Street. A small part of this large house still remains. There was another yard for repair work farther down river very nearly opposite the residence of the shipwright Daniel Short. The Daniel Short house on Hinkley Hill, sometimes called Christian Hill, on the road between Calais and Bog Brook, was built by Captain McGregor and was one of the houses purchased by the Shorts when they moved there from St. Andrews. Cornelius and James Short also resided in Calais, and the other brothers, including John and Charles, lived at St. Stephen.

The firm at St. Stephen was known as J. & C. Short and the Calais company was known as the Short Brothers. They built ships, barques, brigs and other types of sailing craft for Chipman & Bolton, J. S. De Wolf, both of St. Stephen with offices in London and Liverpool, England; other ships were built for J. S. Murchie, Todd Brothers, and others of Calais, Maine; many of the vessels were owned outright by the Short Brothers. After 1878, their active shipbuilding operations at Calais took place just below the city, also at Robbinston, Perry, and Whiting, Maine. Thirty-six vessels have been recorded; those constructed and repaired after 1878 were not recorded. The yards were considered the finest for their repair work along the coast of Maine and New Brunswick, repairing vessels during the winter months for the early spring shipments of lumber from the St. Croix region. Contracts for repair work were made from all along the coast in the autumn, keeping many men employed during the winter months. In one yard so many men carried tin lunch pails that a settlement nearby became known as "Tin Kettle Valley."

After a life of great activity Charles Short passed on at St. Stephen, New Brunswick, in 1895.

The last ship work by Charles Short was moulding the frame of the five-masted barque *Shenandoah* at Bishop's Crossing, Quebec. The vessel was built at Bath, Maine, and was the largest wooden barque afloat at that time.

Other sailing vessels built by the Short Brothers between 1861 and 1878 were: ships, *Cashmere, Sea Chief, Sea Crest, Wolfville;* barques, *Ellen De Wolf, Joseph E. Eaton, John E. Chase, Florence Chipman, Grasmere, Kathleen, Lynton, Marion King, Oswingo, Sea, Windemere;* brigs, *F. H. Todd, Ethel Bolton;* schooners, *Addie Murchie, Almaretta, Elizabeth Cook, Annie Murchie, Georgia Todd, Henry G. Fay, Lettie Wells, Alemeratto, Lottie,* and *Nellie,* these last being jolly schooner names.

John Fitch, the so-called erratic inventor of the first steamboat in this country, was born at Windsor, Connecticut, and later lived on the banks of the Delaware River. Here he invented the plan for rowing a boat with a steam engine which was the first vessel in this country to be successfully steam propelled. It was launched on July 27, 1786, and was Fitch's second experiment with steam and paddles.

This vessel was 45 feet long, with paddles working on each side, and it moved at the rate of four miles an hour. The boiler and machinery were found to be inadequate, so another vessel 60 feet long was built in 1788, with paddles placed at the stern in the same manner that the Chinese paddled their boats by hand.

A later boat built by John Fitch in 1790 made seven miles an hour and was placed in service on the Delaware River. Still later he built the steamboat *Perserverence*.

John Fitch also experimented with propeller boats on Collect Pond, in New York City.

Robert Fulton and his patron, Chancellor Livingstone, have often been credited with introducing steam navigation in this country; there had been several designers who made successful steamboats, but Robert Fulton's second attempt, the *Clermont,* became the most notable of the early experiments in this country.

This steamer is said to have been christened *Katharine of Clermont* in honor of Robert Fulton's wife, who was Chancellor Livingstone's daughter; their residence overlooking the Hudson River was named Clermont.

The *Clermont* was launched in April 1807 from the shipyards of Charles Brown, and was not much larger than a regular canal boat. The vessel was 130 feet long, equipped with fore and aft sails, had a

cross head type engine placed in full view, which burned wood, and the paddle wheels were the so-called Fulton Patent. The engine was imported from England by Jacob Barker, who came from Nantucket Island and became a wealthy merchant with offices in New York and Liverpool.

On August 7, 1807, the *Clermont* made the first trip up the Hudson River to Albany in thirty hours, probably the longest trip of any steamboat at that time. This experimental voyage greatly contributed to the early development of the steamboat. In 1808, the vessel was lengthened and almost wholly rebuilt to accommodate the number of enthusiastic passengers.

The great success of the *Clermont* led Robert Fulton and Chancellor Livingstone to build the boats *The Car of Neptune* and *Paragon*.

In 1816, the *Clermont* was again lengthened: to 150 feet, 13 feet breadth, and 7 feet depth of hold, and renamed *North River*.

Though Robert Fulton was not the inventor of the steamboat in this country, he saw the great possibilities in the development of steam applied to paddle wheels, the combination of both sail and steam, and is entitled to honor for perfecting the steamboat which developed to greater size and tonnage.

Maine, New Brunswick, and Nova Scotia Steamboats and Steamships

It was not long after the *Clermont* plied the Hudson River that Maine could boast of steamboats. The *Thom Thumb* was the first successful steamboat to appear in Maine coastal waters, about 1818. Unfortunately, very little is known about this boat, but it is said to have been a side wheeler and was used on the Kennebec River as an excursion boat. It was later put in regular service between Bath and Augusta, until about 1828. The steamboat *Maine* is said to have been the second steamboat on the Maine Coast, followed by the *Waterville*.

Sixteen years after the first practical application of steam to the propulsion of vessels, the first regular steamboat appeared in the waters of Maine. This was the *Patent* which arrived in Portland July 7, 1823. This boat was built in New York and is said to have made excursions about Boston Harbor before being brought to the Maine Coast by Captain Porter. Within the same year the boat was acquired by the newly organized Kennebec Steam Navigation Company and used from Boston to Bath, Maine.

The steamboat *Maine* is said to have been in service from Bath to Eastport. And about this time the steam packet *New York*, built at Norfolk, Virginia, is said to have been in service along the coast from New York to Eastport, stopping at Portland, Belfast, and intermediate points by agreement.

There were many other steamboats that plied the Maine Coast and rivers in the early days. The steamboat *Eagle* is mentioned on the Saint Croix River, to Calais, Maine, in 1825. The second steamer of Boston Harbor was sold to parties at Eastport, Maine, for use on the Saint Croix River and about Passamaquoddy Bay in 1832.

Later steamboats along the Maine Coast from 1832 to 1900 were the *Legislator, Connecticut, General Knox, Rockland, Cambridge, Charter Oak, City of Rockland, Eastern Queen,* and the *Harvest Moon.*

In 1901, the Kennebec Steamship Company, the Boston and Bangor Steamship Company, organized in 1827, the Portland Steamship Company, organized in 1832, the International Steamship Company, organized in 1845, and other smaller companies were all consolidated under the name of the Eastern Steamship Company of Maine. This company operated regular lines, connecting the principal parts of Maine and New Brunswick with Boston until 1935. The Eastern Steamship Company continued with one boat in service from Boston to Yarmouth, Nova Scotia, during summer months until 1954.

99

A Steamboat Voyage Down East

The Maine and New Brunswick steamboats would leave Boston from Lincoln's or India Wharf late in the afternoon and paddle down the harbor with a proud stateliness and speed, looking down on the many steamers, coasters, yachts, and islands on every side.

The course led out through Broad Sound into Massachusetts Bay, past the Graves Lighthouse with the ragged and rocky Brewster Islands and ledges on the right, the beaches of Winthrop and Lynn on the left, past the hills, islands and villages of the North Shore, Nahant, Swampscott, Manchester, and Gloucester; and the tall stone lighthouses on Thatcher's Island, off the end of Cape Ann, were passed close at hand before the broad sunset came.

The itinerary continued through the night across the Gulf of Maine toward Monhegan Island, whose brilliant light cheered the darkness of early morning; at dawn the steamboat passed Whitehead and entered Penobscot Bay, with its many craggy islands on the right, including Dix Island, from which the famous granite used in constructing so many Government buildings in Washington, D. C., has come.

Soon after rounding the picturesque promontory of Owl's Head, the boat docked at Rockland, Maine, at five o'clock in the morning. Here connections were made with the Mount Desert boat, and fourteen other small steamers awaiting passengers for various islands. The big steamboat next paddled up the bay toward the noble Blue Hills of Camden, Maine, which inspired the beautiful poem, "I Saw Three Hills," by Edna St. Vincent Millay. A stop was made at this seaport town which has often been called "The Jewel of the Penobscot."

The next landing was at Northport and from beyond this place the steamboat emerged from the thronging islands of Penobscot Bay and paddled across a large lake-like inner harbor to the handsome maritime city of Belfast, whose fine old houses rise in an imposing line

101

along the hill at the mouth of the Passagassawaukeag River; this beautiful city was settled in 1770, by Scotch-Irish Presbyterians.

After leaving Belfast, occasional glimpses of historic old Castine were obtained at the far right across the bay where historic memories were recalled: Plymouth Pilgrims, Cardinal Richelieu's gay French soldiers, the wars of D'Aulney and Latour, the feudal rule of the Baron de St. Castin, the long occupation by garrisons of red-coated British infantry, and the blockade of a great American fleet by a half-dozen intrepid English frigates.

About five miles above Belfast the steamboat rounded in under the lee of Brigadier Island and landed at the wonderful old bayside village of Searsport, the vast domain and islands once owned by David Sears of Boston. For a long period this port was known far and wide for its sea captains and for the fine sailing ships built there.

Once more the steamer paddled out into the bay, the long peninsula of Castine visible on the eastward, crowned with the earthworks of Fort George.

The next stopping place was Fort Point. There were the ruins of Fort Pownal, which was built in 1758 by Governor Pownal of Massachusetts, when Maine was Massachusetts, at the cost of the British Parliament, to defend the entrance of the Penobscot River. Seventeen years later a British frigate sailed here and opened fire, and the Blue Jackets destroyed the works and levelled the parapets of this important fortification.

After leaving Fort Point, our boat paddled up the famous Penobscot River whose sources lie hundreds of miles inland amidst a deer-haunted wilderness gleaming with bright lakes, where no navigation but that of a canoe has ever been attempted.

Paddling around through the rapid currents of the Bucksport Narrows, the most difficult achievement of the entire voyage, the steamboat advanced to the wharf at Bucksport, a beautiful old village of shipbuilders, farmers, and fishermen. On the opposite shore rose the massive, frowning walls of Fort Knox which was a modern structure erected by the Government to seal up the Penobscot River against hostile ships, and to protect the one-time vast shipping of lumber from Bangor. About five miles upriver was the landing at Winterport.

As the boat paddled on, the river grew more narrow and sinuous, with picturesque highlands near its banks and scattered farms of the hardy country people of Maine.

The steamboat would pass many kinds of sailing craft bound in and out which were the indications of prosperous commerce. A short

102

stop was made at Hampden, which was captured by the British fleet in 1814. A few miles beyond, the steamboat reached the terminal point, Bangor, twenty leagues from the sea and crowning a line of graceful hills; here one could take a train for points in central and western Maine, also within the Maritime Provinces.

At Rockland, Maine, the staunch and swift steamboat *Mount Desert* and later the *J. T. Morse* would meet the "Boston Boat" which usually arrived very early in the morning, and would then paddle across Penobscot Bay to the central group of islands and pass through the charming scenery of Fox Island Thoroughfare, touching at several quaint maritime villages and giving superb views of the Camden Mountains, also the remote seaward cliffs of Isle au Haut and the bold peaks of Mount Desert.

After crossing Placemtia Bay the steamboat visited Bass Harbor and Southwest Harbor, rounded the bold eastern headland of Mount Desert, and paddled into Frenchman's Bay by a long line of spray white cliffs and many villas, then went on to Bar Harbor, a once fabulous summer resort; the course extended farther to the head of the bay, Sullivan. This trip across Penobscot Bay was one of the most interesting and beautiful along the entire Atlantic Coast, rich in variety of marine and coastal scenery, with lighthouses, straits and bays, grand mountains, and invigorating sea breezes sweeping over all. The steamboats *Mount Desert* and *J. T. Morse* were renowned for speed and seaworthy qualities which always made the trips enjoyable ones.

The greater part of the voyage lead through an endless labyrinth of islands and rocks, along narrow passages swept by the salt tides, across sheltered bays and fjords, giving one the greatest imaginable variety of scenic effects in a journey filled with brilliant interest. The seaside villages at which the steamboats stopped had great attractions for one who delighted in out-of-the-way localities which formed an effective contrast to the modern villages, resorts, and hotels.

This eastward voyage and those to the most eastern points of Maine and New Brunswick, traversing the vast quiet reaches of the sea in the bracing salt air, afforded a change of scene and life which was always rich, interesting and rewarding; and so today we treasure pleasant thoughts of Old Steamboat Days on the Coast of Maine and New Brunswick.

Steamboat	*Eagle*
	Built in 1817

Captains:
  James Moorfield
  Lemuel Clark of Plymouth, Massachusetts
  Barnabas Lincoln of Hingham, Massachusetts
  John Wood of Salem, Massachusetts
Pilot: George Beal

Steamboat *Eagle,* unofficially named *John Hancock* at its launching on April 9, 1817, was built by Gilbert Brewster of Norwich, Connecticut, with a small engine and wooden boiler. He prepared the vessel for an excursion on the Thames River; fifty passengers went on board and the steamboat paddled to New London, Connecticut, on this trial trip. While all passengers were on the upper deck viewing the arrival of the steamboat *Fulton* with President Monroe on board, the wooden boiler exploded. The vessel was rebuilt with two copper boilers, her tonnage increased, and, when just a year old, she left Long Island Sound and was the first steamboat to cross to Nantucket Island, Massachusetts.

The first trip was made from New Bedford to Nantucket on May 5, 1818, taking about sixty passengers, and the fastest trip the steamboat made was eight hours and seven minutes, about twice the time of the present-day steamers. It was considered fast and seaworthy at that time, but the loss in operating this wood-burning vessel was so huge and travel so infrequent due to the smart sailing packets, that after one season, the boat was sold to the Boston & Hingham Steamboat Company, a forerunner of the present Nantasket Line. This boat made trips from Boston to Salem, Massachusetts, via Marblehead, landing at Crowinshield's Wharf, where a house had been erected for the steamboat passengers and storage space for their luggage. But travel continued to be light because of stern warnings of stagecoach companies as to the risk and dangers of new steam contraptions, so the Salem trips were discontinued.

Steamboat *Eagle* resumed regular trips to Hingham, Nahant, and Plymouth, Massachusetts, until 1824, at which time it was sold to parties at Passamaquoddy, now Eastport, Maine. This rugged little boat paddled the coast of Maine, stopping at intermediate points for wood refueling. The boat paddled the Saint Croix River and landed at a wharf near the city of Calais, later proceeded to Saint John, New Brunswick, and is probably the first steamboat placed on an international line.

In spite of the diminutive size of this boat, it was a successful experiment, though the stage companies and smart sailing packets were strong competitors for many years. It will be seen from the picture that the *Eagle* was beautifully designed for an early steamboat, with a figurehead representing Neptune's Trident, a hog frame, a rounded stern, and a cross head type of engine.

The *Eagle* was sold in 1828 at Passamaquoddy, but was not used in regular service much longer due to its weakened condition after an adventurous career of twenty years. It was broken up and abandoned along the St. Croix River near Calais, where its bones now rest in a marsh inlet.

The *Eagle* was 92 feet long,
17 feet beam, 6½ feet depth of hold;
80 tons register, later increased to 104 tons.

Savannah

Built in 1818
Captain Robert Innott of Nantucket Island
Captain Moses Rogers of New London, Conn.

The *Savannah,* built at Corlear's Hook, New York, by Crocker & Fickett, was launched on August 22, 1818. It was built as a sailing packet to ply between New York and Liverpool, but was purchased soon after the launching to be rebuilt as a side-wheel steamer for transatlantic service between Savannah and Liverpool.

The complete rigging remained, and a steam engine was added with a removable shaft and paddle wheels. The latter were constructed like fans so that they could be removed and folded upon the deck when not in use. The wheelhouse was made of canvas stretched on an iron frame. The engine was built by James Pallavre of New York, and was an incline direct-acting single cylinder type engine, 40 inches in diameter, with a 5-foot stroke, and two circular boilers built by Daniel Dodge.

The *Savannah's* speed under steam alone was five knots, and it consumed nine tons of coal a day.

A trial trip was made from New York to Savannah in seven days under Captain Robert Innott's command, relying mostly on sails. After this trip the owners thought there was no doubt that the vessel would accomplish a fast transatlantic voyage, and on May 26, 1819, under Captain Moses Rogers' command, the vessel sailed from Savannah for Liverpool. Carrying neither passengers nor cargo, the ship made nine to ten knots and arrived at Liverpool in twenty-five days. The engine was in use eighteen days during the voyage.

When this side-wheeler arrived on June 20, 1819, with sails furled, and Stars and Stripes flying, all the piers were thronged with thousands of people loudly cheering a vociferous welcome. While in Liverpool the ship was carefully watched by the English authorities, it being

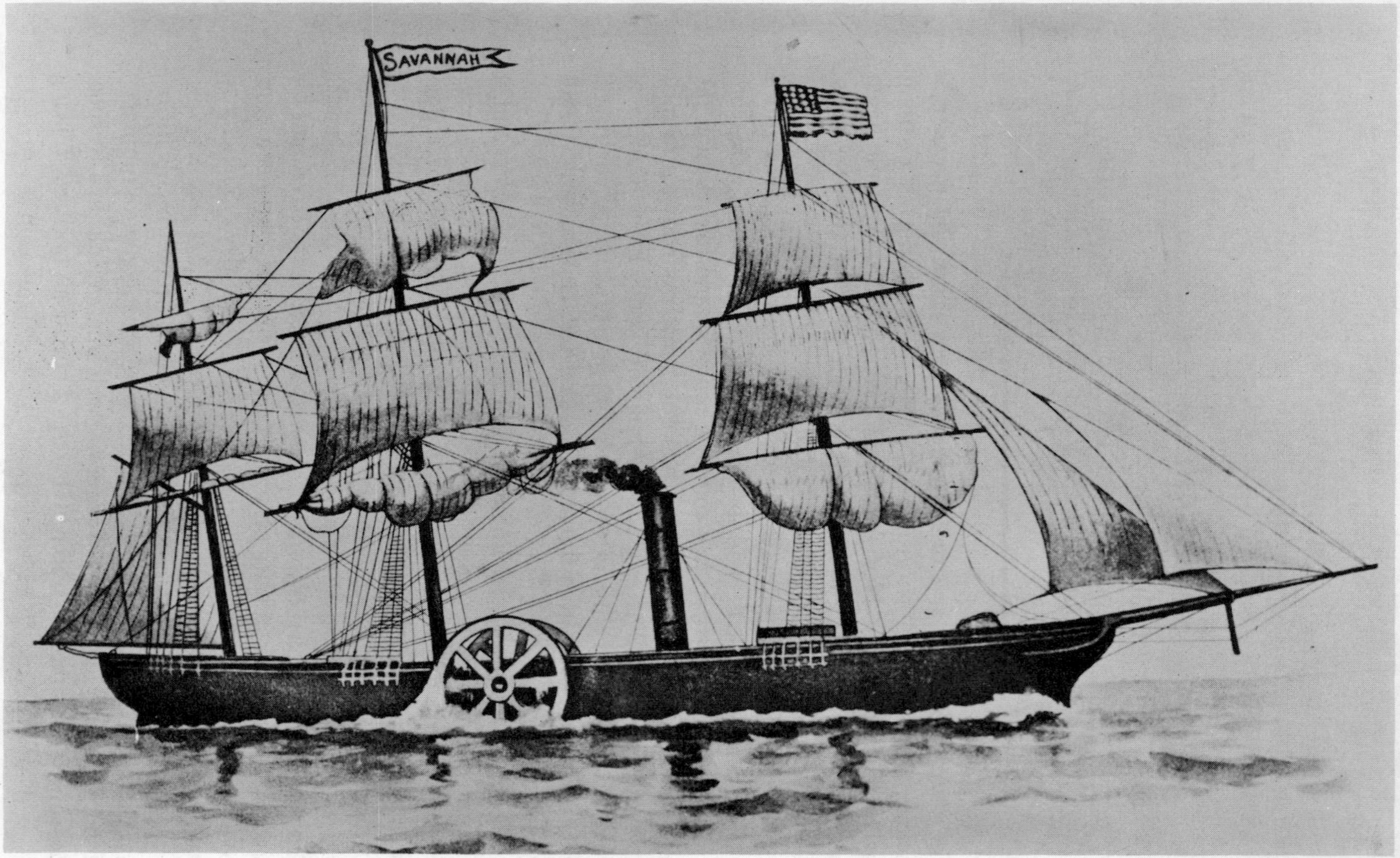

From the Authors' Collection

supposed that the *Savannah* was part of a scheme to carry off Napoleon from the Island of St. Helena.

The vessel then sailed for St. Petersburg in August, 1819, returning to Savannah early in November via Copenhagen and Arendal in Norway. The steamship encountered a very heavy storm on this return trip, but made the voyage in fifty-three days.

On a later trip from Savannah to Washington, the *Savannah* lost its lifeboats and anchors off Cape Hatteras. Later, after it was sold for a sailing packet between New York and Savannah, the vessel grounded on one of these voyages, became a complete loss, and was broken up.

It is the sailing of the *Savannah* in 1819 that is commemorated throughout the United States on May 22nd as National Maritime Day.

The *Savannah* was 130 feet long,
26 feet breadth, 16½ feet depth of hold;
380 tons gross.

Note:

This steamboat has been included in this book having made such a world contribution in the development of steam and sail navigation combined.

Steamboat

Lafayette

Built in 1824
Captain Luce
Captain Thaxter of Hingham, Massachusetts

The *Lafayette* was built at Mt. Holly, New Jersey, in 1824, and was so named because General Lafayette visited the United States that year. This boat was a very crude model of about 60 tons register with a beam engine made partly of wood. It had one deck, one small wood-burning boiler and so little power that trips to Nantucket Island could not be made unless weather conditions were most favorable. Even then at times it could not paddle around Brant Point against the tide.

This little steamboat was first in service at Lamberton, New Jersey, and in 1829 it was enrolled at New Bedford for the Nantucket service, being the second steamboat to Nantucket Island, the second to Plymouth, Massachusetts, and the second steamboat of the most easterly waters of Maine and New Brunswick. Its name was unofficially changed to *Hamilton,* which was painted on the paddle wheel boxes while in Nantucket service, but the name *Lafayette* always remained on the stern.

Apparently a failure on the Nantucket Line, the boat was sold to the Boston & Hingham Steamboat Company, following the steamboat *Eagle* and resuming the official name of *Lafayette,* which was again painted on the paddle wheel boxes. This boat continued in service from Boston to Hingham until 1832, when it was rebuilt. Thereafter this courageous little steamboat paddled the Maine coast and was registered at Passamaquoddy, now Eastport. It also made trips up the St. Croix River to Calais, Maine, landing at a wharf near the city; it is said to have made a through trip to St. John, New Brunswick.

This portrait was painted by Fred Pansing, and shows that the *Lafayette* did not have masts or sails at a time when steam was not wholly trusted. The through trips from Boston to Passamaquoddy were made by steam alone, which was quite an adventure at that time; the *Eagle* and the *Lafayette* are thought to have had really successful careers as pioneer steamboats of New England. Ezekiel Foster at Passamaquoddy was the owner of *Lafayette* in 1832.

It is assumed that this vessel was broken up at Eastport in 1835.

The *Lafayette* was 68 tons after the rebuilding at Boston. Length of vessel not known.

111

Steamboat

Bangor

Built in 1834
Captain George Barker
Captain Samuel H. Howse
Captain J. Dunn

The steamboat *Bangor,* a heavy, well-constructed boat, was built by Brown & Bell Company, of New York, with fore and aft masts and sails, and equipped with two wood-burning boilers, two stacks, a cross head type of engine with a cylinder 36 inches in diameter and a 9-foot stroke; this engine was considered quite remarkable. Passenger accommodations were comfortable, but the freight capacity was small due to space used for 25 cords of wood fueling.

This boat was considered fast at that time and ran on the Boston-Bangor route until 1840, then was placed in service from Portland to Calais, Maine. Later the *Bangor* was converted to coal burning boilers, was sold in 1842 to Turkish interests at Constantinople, and renamed *Sudower.*

Sudower was used for passenger service from Constantinople to the Prince's Island in the Sea of Marmara. After many years of service for the Turkish Government the boat was broken up.

The *Bangor* was 160 feet long; 400 tons.

PORTLAND.

Steamboat   *Portland I*

Built in 1834
Captain J. B. Coyle, owner, manager,
    and the first engineer
Captain J. Howes
Captain Samuel Stanwood

The *Portland* was built by Nathan Dyer, Jr., at Portland, Maine, in 1834, for the Cumberland Steam Navigation Company. It was very solid and seaworthy, with the cross head type of engines which were taken from the steamboat *Chancellor Livingston* that had been dismantled at Portland during the previous year. It was the first steamboat on the coast of Maine to burn anthracite coal, but was a very slow boat.

The first trip to Boston was made in August of 1835; thereafter it was used on the Boston to Portland route, connecting with the steamboat *Bangor I*. This steamer also made trips to Bangor, Maine.

After having been somewhat rebuilt and having a second mast added, the *Portland* was sold to James Cunningham of New York in 1842, and later sold to Isaac Newton in 1844. In 1847, this boat was chartered by the United States Government for war service during the Mexican War and was sent to New Orleans.

After leaving New Orleans with troops and supplies, the *Portland* encountered a terrific storm, and about 100 horses had to be thrown overboard to save the troops, crew, and supplies.

At the close of the the war the steamboat was bought by Harris & Morgan of New Orleans and placed in service from New Orleans to Texas ports. The *Portland* was wrecked at La Salle, Texas, in 1854.

The *Portland* was 163 feet long,
    27 feet breadth, 10½ feet depth of hold;
    400 tons.

Steamboat

John W. Richmond

Built in 1838
Captain William N. Townsend
John Babcock, agent

The *John W. Richmond* was built by Colonel John Body of Eddy's Point, Providence, Rhode Island, and was named for Dr. John W. Richmond. It started regular trips from Providence to New York on June 1, 1838.

A famous steamboat race on Long Island Sound took place between the *John W. Richmond* and the *Lexington,* starting from Stonington, Connecticut. The *Lexington* is said to have been the finer and faster of the two, but the *Richmond* steamed and boiled ahead and won the race into New York harbor.

About 1839, the *John W. Richmond* was sold and used on the coast of Maine, running from Boston to Bath, Gardiner, and Hallowell; it was destroyed by fire in 1843, at Hallowell, Maine. *Penobscot I* followed on this line.

The *John W. Richmond* was 210 feet long, 28 feet breadth, 10 feet depth of hold; 320 tons.

Penobscot I and Kennebec II

Built 1843	Built 1845
Captains:	Captains:
Samuel Seymour	Edward H. Sanford
T. B. Sanford	Charles O. Clark
Nathaniel Kimball	William Flowers
Thomas G. Jewett	

Kennebec II and *Penobscot I* were owned by the Kennebec Steamboat Company and controlled by Captain Menemon Sanford. They were very similar in design and construction, the wooden hulls being painted black and the upper decks white; both boats were equipped with vertical beam engines with 41 inch cylinders and 11-foot stroke; the paddle wheel boxes were decorative.

The hull of the *Kennebec* was built by Bishop & Simonson of Philadelphia, and the engines were built by T. F. Secor & Company, New York. Stanton and Spicer were the original owners of *Kennebec II* which was placed on the Boston, Bath, and Hallowell run until 1849, when it was placed on the Bangor line.

The first trip of *Penobscot I,* commanded by Captain Jewett, on June 17, 1845, followed what was known as the outside route for the first time; this route is the direct course from Cape Ann to Monhegan Island, and had never before been attempted by a steamboat commander; the course has been used extensively since that time.

Both of these steamboats were registered at Bath and later sold for service between New York, Cape May, and Philadelphia. *Penobscot* was the first one sold, and renamed *City of Norfolk*. This boat was lost in a heavy gale off the coast of Delaware in September of 1857. *Kennebec* followed on the New York-Cape May Line and was in service until destroyed by fire in 1870.

The *Penobscot* was 196 feet long, 26 feet breadth, 10½ feet depth of hold; 494 tons.

The *Kennebec* was 212 feet long, 26½ feet breadth, 10½ feet depth of hold; 480 tons.

Steamboat   *T. F. Secor*

Built in 1846
Captain Sanford

The *T. F. Secor* was built at New York in 1846 by the T. F. Secor Company for the Belfast, Ellsworth, and Bar Harbor, Maine, route, connecting with the Boston Boat at Belfast. It was probably the second vertical beam engine steamer in eastern Maine, the others being the cross head type.

The artist of this primitive portrait has brought out the simple lines and detail of this amusing little steamer. The *Secor* had a vertical beam engine, plain paddle wheel boxes, and a single stack. It was painted all white with gaily colored trimmings.

In 1863, the boat was sold to the United States Government for war service in the Civil War and was later destroyed by fire.

The *T. F. Secor* was 130 feet long; 210 tons.

Steamboat

State of Maine II
Built in 1881
Captain S. F. Pike
Captain Hilyard

There were only two steamboats named *State of Maine;* the first one was built at New York by Bishop & Simonson in 1848 especially for the Eastern and Boston and Maine Railroads, and was registered at Bangor. This steamboat was by far the largest and best equipped boat ever seen along the coast up to that time.

State of Maine I was built with a vertical beam engine, with 11-foot stroke, a 54 inch cylinder, twin smoke stacks, and two iron boilers placed on the guards, because passengers still feared boiler explosions, and this was considered a great safety precaution. This boat proved much too large and expensive for the Maine coast run and was sold to the Fall River Line and placed in service from New York to Fall River until chartered by the United States Government in 1860. Later this boat was in service on the Hudson River and about New York Harbor, and was still registered in 1872. The signal letters were H. R. K. F. This boat was 248 feet long, 32 feet breadth, 840 gross tons, and 760 net tons.

The well-known *State of Maine* the second was built by the New England Shipbuilding Company at Bath, in 1881, for the International Steamboat Company, and was registered at Eastport.

This all-wood side-wheel boat was exceptionally well constructed, the hull being built much like a ship with frames close together. The engine was a vertical beam, of 1,200 horse power; there were twin smoke stacks, fore and aft masts equipped with sails; the half-moon shaped paddle wheel boxes were decorated with a fan-shaped pattern and a border of stars; the State of Maine seal polychromed was placed in the center of each; a handsomely carved and gilded eagle gleamed

122

from the top of the pilot house. *State of Maine* was used in alternating service with steamboat *Cumberland,* a boat similar in size and design, on the so-called inside line, Boston, Bangor and Mt. Desert, and sometimes made trips to St. John, New Brunswick. Mr. Edward Cushing of Camden, Maine, was General Manager of this line when these two steamboats were in service.

In 1902, both of these boats were sold to the well-known Joy Line for regular service between New York and Providence, being registered at Hartford. *State of Maine* was renamed *Edgemont,* the *Cumberland* was renamed *Larchmont.* The *Edgemont* was again sold for service from New York to Cape May, later was condemned and in 1924 was broken up.

This boat was manned by a crew of sixty-five while in Maine coastal waters. This interesting portrait is by Antonio Jacobsen. The signal letters were J. W. G. K. There is now the training ship *State of Maine* at the Maritime Academy at Castine.

The *State of Maine* II was 241 feet long, 37 feet breadth, 14 feet depth of hold; 1,736 gross tons and 1,145 net tons.

Steamboat   *Ocean*

Built in 1849
Captain T. B. Sanford

The *Ocean* was built by Lawrence & Faulkes at New York for Captain Menemon Sanford, first registered at Bath, Maine, and placed in service from Boston to Bath. This was the largest and fastest boat to be used on the Sanford's Line up to that time.

The *Ocean* had a beam engine, twin funnels, and perfectly rigged fore and aft sails; the boilers were placed on the outer guards for safety. There was a gold eagle placed over the bell between the funnels, and a sunburst decoration was painted on the so-called half-moon shaped paddle wheel boxes, with an "eye" painted in the center of each to enable the boat to see; this idea was taken from the early Chinese vessels and was applied to a number of steamboats.

On November 24, 1854, the *Ocean,* while entering Boston Harbor, was rammed by the Cunard steamship *Canada* which was outward bound. The shock of the collision upset the lights and stoves on board the *Ocean.* The boat burned and sank at the same time. Five passengers jumped overboard and were drowned, but over a hundred other passengers were rescued by nearby boats in the harbor.

This interesting portrait was painted by James Bard about whom a biography appears in the appendix of this volume.

The steamboat *Governor* followed the *Ocean* on the Boston-Bath Line until the *Eastern Queen,* built especially for the service, was completed.

> The *Ocean* was 223 feet long,
> 28 feet breadth, 11 feet depth of hold;
> 658 tons.

Daniel Webster

Built in 1853

Captains:

Deering   Otis Ingraham

Samuel Blanchard   William R. Roix

The steamboat *Daniel Webster* was built by Samuel Sneeden & Company of New York in 1853 for the Boston-St. John Service, taking both passengers and freight. This boat, like many others of the period, was designed and built with fore and aft masts and a vertical beam engine; the boilers were placed on the outer guards, which was considered a great safety precaution at the time; a fan-shaped pattern decorated the large paddle wheel boxes on both sides; the signal letters were H. F. D. K.

This steamboat was considered fast, elegant, and seaworthy, with excellent accommodations for passengers, having 42 staterooms and 200 berths. The saloon was luxuriously furnished for a steamboat of the times. A life-size portrait of the famed statesman in a gold frame was presented by some of Daniel Webster's friends and it hung in the saloon of the boat; later it was owned by a family of Bath, Maine.

At the beginning of the Civil War the *Daniel Webster* was taken over by the United States Government and used as a hospital ship. At the close of the war, this boat and the steamboat *Cossack* were purchased by a Boston steamboat company and owned by Spear, Lang & Delano; the *Cossack*, renamed *Eastern City*, had been in service from Portland to Bangor before the war. These two steamboats were placed in an opposition line to the Kennebec River.

The steamboat *Rockland* first by name, connected with the steamboat *Daniel Webster* at Rockland, Maine, when the latter was on the Boston-St. John Line; the *Rockland* took passengers to the various islands of Penobscot Bay, also to Blue Hill, Bar Harbor, Sullivan and Machias; the steamboats *Mount Desert* and *J. T. Morse* were later put in service on the Rockland-Bar Harbor route.

About 1863, the *Daniel Webster* was sold for service on the St. Lawrence River, and the name was changed to *Saguenay;* this steamboat was not exceeded by any Down East passenger boat until the launching of the side-wheel boat *Katahdin* in 1863. J. T. Morse was the owner of the *Daniel Webster* in 1883.

> The *Daniel Webster* was 240 feet long, 34 feet breadth, 11 feet depth of hold; 910 tons.

Steamboat   *Forest City*

Built in 1854
Captain Richard Donovan

The *Forest City* was built at Greenpoint, Long Island, New York, by John Englis & Sons Company for the Portland, Maine, Steam Packet Company. It may be seen from this portrait by Antonio Jacobsen that this was a side-wheel boat with a beam engine, a single stack and fore and aft sails. It was painted white all over with brightly colored deck rails.

When the Confederates raided Portland Harbor the *Forest City* was immediately armed and sent out in pursuit of the raiders, some of whom were captured. This steamboat remained in service from Boston to Portland until 1894, when, after a forty-year career, it was sold and broken up. The signal letters were H. G. T. W.

The *Forest City* was 234 feet long, 33 feet breadth, 12 feet depth of hold; 1,134 gross tons and 1,072 net tons.

Steamer

Menemon Sanford

Built in 1854
Captain Charles B. Sanford

The *Menemon Sanford* was built at Greenpoint, New York, by John Englis & Sons Company, especially for service from New York to Cape May and Philadelphia.

About 1856, the *Sanford* was placed on the Boston-Bangor line. It was painted all white with gaily colored deck rails, and had a vertical beam engine, single stack, fore and aft masts with sails.

This steamboat ran aground on Thatchers Island off Cape Ann, Gloucester, on the morning of July 5, 1856. The cause of the accident is said to have been the result of a Fourth of July celebration of the officers. Due to favorable weather conditions and great skill in chopping away part of the boat, it was possible to place the vessel back in service again.

The *Menemon Sanford* ran ashore again in a thick fog near the scene of the first accident, but was pulled off in safety. This boat was soon chartered by the United States Government for Civil War service at New Orleans. Later the *Sanford* again ran ashore, this time on the coast of Florida, and was a total loss.

The *Menemon Sanford* was 247 feet long, 34 feet breadth, 12 feet depth of hold; 1,000 tons.

Steamboat ### *John Brooks*

Built in 1859
Captain J. J. Liscomb
Captain E. W. Davidson

The *John Brooks* was built at New York in 1859 and was first used on the New York-Bridgeport Line. It was a side-wheeler with a vertical beam engine, schooner-rigged with fore and aft sails, originally built with two boilers on the guards, and painted white all over with green trimming.

This steamboat was chartered during the Civil War for $600.00 a day, and served in Virginia and Carolina waters; later it was in service from Boston to Plymouth during the summer months.

In 1865, the *John Brooks* was purchased by the Portland Steam Packet Company, and placed on the Boston-Portland route. At this time it was somewhat rebuilt and converted to one boiler with a 1,000 horsepower engine. It still remained a very fast boat, and is said to have made trips as far as Eastport and St. John, New Brunswick.

In 1890, the *Brooks* was purchased by the Boston-Portsmouth Steamboat Company, registered at Boston, and placed in service from Boston to Portsmouth, stopping at the Isles of Shoals during the summer months until 1898. The signal letters were H. L. R. K.

The *John Brooks* was 275 feet long, 31 feet breadth, 10 feet depth of hold; 1,011 gross tons and 916 net tons.

133

Penobscot II

Built in 1882
Captain Otis Ingraham
Captain William Gates

Penobscot II was built by Messrs. Smith & Townsend at East Boston, Massachusetts, in 1882. The beam engine of 1,200 horsepower, having a 12-foot stroke and a cylinder 58 inches in diameter, was built by the well-known Atlantic Works, also at East Boston. *Penobscot* had a single stack, fore and aft masts with sails, as steam was not wholly trusted even at this period. Its signal letters were J. W. D. L., and it had a crew of sixty-five.

Architectural detail and panelling of this boat was very pleasing, the half-moon shaped paddle wheel boxes were most decorative with a portrait of a Penobscot Indian placed in the center of each. The passenger accommodations were de luxe for the times, and *Penobscot* was the second boat to paddle the Gulf of Maine with electric lights, as it was equipped with a dynamo. The engine room was of spectacular beauty, the polished steel and brasses being always well kept; and the large crank attached to the beam engine as well as the paddle wheels were painted bright red.

Great efforts were made by the owners to make *Penobscot* the finest of all Maine coast steamboats, but the boat proved to be much too wide, slow, heavy, and cumbersome for river navigation in winter; after later reconstruction it was improved, but remained hard to steer.

Penobscot was first registered at Boston, later at Bath, and placed in alternating service with steamboat *Kennebec III* on the Boston-Bangor Line. In 1901, the boat was sold to the well-known Joy Line and placed in service from New York to Providence; later it was sold for service on the Hudson River, and renamed *Mohawk*.

While paddling on the Hudson River *Mohawk* was in several accidents; twice grounded, tugged off the flats, repaired, repainted, and replaced in regular service. In 1915, the boat was again sold, rebuilt as a sailing vessel, principally for the transportation of coal. After being in service for about thirty-three years in all, it was lost at sea with all men on board.

This portrait after the lithograph by Currier and Ives was reproduced from a painting by R. Pearson.

The *Penobscot* was 255 feet long,
38 feet breadth, 13 feet depth of hold;
1,414 gross tons and 1,244 net tons.

Steamboat

Golden Rod
Built in 1893

The small steamer *Golden Rod* was built at Brewer, Maine, in 1893, registered at Bangor, and first used on the "Round the Hills" service from Hancock to Sorrento, Bar Harbor, Northeast Harbor, and Southwest Harbor. This popular little propeller steamer, equipped with a 50 horsepower engine, was painted white with dark green deck rails and was generally known as the "Rud". The "Rud" was later transferred to Penobscot Bay and was travelled on by residents and visitors of this region for many years. It also became the daily mail boat, traversing the bay from Castine to West Brooksville, Islesboro, Camden, Belfast, and Castine. This little boat seemed to set the pace of the village life of Castine, as the mailbag was always most important; everything depended on what time the "Rud" came in and what time the "Rud" left for Belfast.

The *Golden Rod* was manned by four during the summer months and at other times by only two. The "Rud" had a real personality, as hospitable as the engineer's, who would invite early morning passengers to the boiler room for coffee, doughtnuts, and an egg done the way anyone wished.

This interesting photograph made from one of the old glass plates shows the "Rud" approaching the old steamboat wharf at Bar Harbor. The summer mansion in the right background has been remodelled as a hotel.

Steamer *Golden Rod* was last listed in the Register of 1929, indicating that the boat was not in service after that time; its bones now rest along the shore at Castine. Some of the old seafaring folk have it that "the 'Rud' hailed from Castine and died at Castine," though the boat had been registered at Bangor, Bucksport, and Belfast as well.

The *Golden Rod* was 75 feet long,
15 feet breadth, 6 feet depth of hold;
71 gross tons and 52 net tons.

137

Steamboat *Adelaide*

Built in 1854
Captain E. B. Winchester

The *Adelaide* was built at Greenpoint, in New York expressly for the Calais Steamboat Company, which was formed in 1851. This company placed the steamers *Eastern City* and *Adelaide* on the alternating route from Boston to St. John, calling at Portland and Eastport.

Both steamers were wooden side-wheelers, and were very nearly the same size; *The Eastern City,* built in 1852, was slightly larger, being 226 feet long, 30 feet breadth and 10 feet depth of hold. Each steamboat had a vertical beam engine with 44-inch cylinder and 11-foot stroke.

The *Adelaide* was painted all white with fore and aft sails; the paddle wheel boxes were elaborately decorated with a full-length portrait of Queen Adelaide in the center of each one. This boat was considered a very beautiful one and remained in service for many years.

During the Civil War this steamboat was used as a transport, remaining in use until about 1880.

The *Adelaide* was 224 feet long,
28 feet breadth and 8 feet depth of hold;
734 tons.

City of Portland

Built in 1860
Captain S. H. Pike

The *City of Portland,* formerly the *New England,* was built at Portland, Maine, in 1860, by the International Steamship Company. It was an all wood side-wheel boat with a vertical beam engine, twin stacks, fore and aft sails. The vessel was used on the Boston, Portland, Eastport, and St. John run, and also other routes along the Maine Coast.

In this portrait by Antonio Jacobsen the "Union Jack" will be observed on the foremast, as well as our own flag on the aft mast.

The *City of Portland* ran ashore on the coast of Maine in 1872 and was badly damaged. It was rebuilt and placed in service, only to run aground again in 1884, becoming a complete loss to the owners.

The *City of Portland* was 240 feet long, 32 feet breadth, 14 feet depth of hold; 1,026 tons.

THE "BRAVE OLD" KEARSARGE

From the Authors' Collection

Sloop of War *Kearsarge*
Built in 1861

This vessel, known as the Brave Old *Kearsarge,* is considered the most famous ship built in Maine. It was launched at Kittery Navy Yard on September 11, 1861, and is said to have been christened by one of the Kearsarge family of New Hampshire. The hull was of wood brought from Mt. Kearsarge, New Hampshire, and mounted with seven guns.

Two-cylinder, horizontal engines were built by Woodruf & Beach of Hartford, Connecticut, especially for the *Kearsarge.* The commander was John Anicrum Winslow, and the chief engineer a Mr. Cushman. The crew of one hundred and sixty-three mechanics and seamen were all from the New England coast.

A most famous naval battle between the *Kearsarge* and the *Alabama* took place near Cherbourg, France, in 1864, in which the *Kearsarge,* serving the Union, destroyed and sank the Confederate warship.

After the close of the Civil War, the *Kearsarge* continued in use as a steamer; although there was some reconstruction made from time to time, the vessel remained practically the same until lost on Roncador Reef in the Caribbean Sea, off the coast of Nicaragua, on February 2, 1894.

The *Kearsarge* was 221 feet long,
34 feet breadth, 16 feet depth of hold;
1,031 tons.

Rose Standish

Built in 1863
Captain George Beal of Hingham, Massachusetts
Captain Daniel Ryan of Calais, Maine

The *Rose Standish* was built by Messrs. Lawrence & Faulkes at Brooklyn, New York, in 1863, and was registered at Hingham, Massachusetts, being the sixth boat built and placed in service for the Boston, Hingham, and Nantasket Steamboat Company; this boat had accommodations for 1,000 passengers.

On August 28, 1884, the vessel was rammed by a tugboat in Boston Harbor and sank; it was soon raised, reconditioned, and again placed in regular service. Three years later the *Rose,* as the boat was generally called, was sold to the Frontier Steamboat Company of Calais.

There was much excitement on the arrival of this boat in Down East waters. The *Rose* was a fine, elegant, and fast steamer with a comfortably furnished saloon on the upper deck, and was considered a great improvement over former boats used on the St. Croix River Line, such as the *Ellie Knight, Belle Brown* and the *Charles Houghton.* The *Rose* was used for both passengers and freight, as well as excursions; when the tide was low the vessel landed at the lower wharf on the river, and when the tide was high, she could paddle to the main wharf of the city.

After thirteen years of traversing Passamaquoddy Bay and the beautiful river, the steamer was burned at the so-called lower wharf, while it was up on blocks for the winter months of 1900.

This portrait by Fred Pansing shows the side-wheel boat as it was originally built, with a beam engine, open foredeck and awning, and a carved and gilded eagle gleaming from the pilot house. A conventional design graced the paddle wheel boxes. After the boat was raised from Boston Harbor, these decorations were changed to fan-shaped patterns with a female head. Both panels, one of which had been preserved in a private collection, were saved from destruction after the fire in Calais.

The *Rose Standish* was the last side-wheeler to be used on the St. Croix River. It is said that after a time the hull became waterlogged, the paddle wheels set lower in the water, and the boat slowed down considerably. The small propeller boat, *Henry F. Eaton,* followed on the River Line.

The *Rose Standish* was 154 feet long, 27 feet in breadth, 8 feet depth of hold; 392 tons.

145

Steamboat   *Katahdin*
                   Built in 1863
                   Captain Charles B. Sanford

The *Katahdin,* named after the highest mountain in the State of Maine, was built at Brooklyn, New York, by the well-known firm of John Englis & Company in 1863, at a cost of $250,000.00.

This photograph shows the vessel approaching the wharf at Bangor. The *Katahdin* was a side-wheeler, with a vertical beam engine. It had a single stack with fore and aft sails, which were a reassurance to many passengers at that time, who thought steam navigation still an interesting experiment. The boat was painted all white, with bright-colored trimmings, and a fan pattern was painted on the paddle wheel boxes with the seal of the State of Maine in the center of each.

The *Katahdin* stopped at intermediate points en route from Portland to Bangor, including Northport and Sullivan. It is also said to have been in service on the Fall River Line at intervals.

This boat was noted for its seventy staterooms, with 150 men's berths, and 60 berths in the ladies' cabins.

It remained in service until about 1895, when it was sold and broken up.

> The *Katahdin* was 241 feet long,
> 35 feet breadth;
> 1,234 tons.

Steamboat   *Sagadahoc*
Built in 1866
Captain John Collins

The *Sagadahoc,* originally *Star of the East,* was built in New York by John Englis in 1866, for service between Bath, Gardiner, and Hallowell, Maine. The vessel was so large, however, that it could not pass the drawbridge at Gardiner, and this town became the terminus.

In 1889, this boat was rebuilt and renamed the *Sagadahoc.* The boat continued in service on the Maine coast and rivers until sold with its companion steamer, the *Kennebec,* to New York parties for use on the Hudson River.

The *Sagadahoc* was then renamed the *Greenpoint,* and the *Kennebec* was renamed the *Iroquois.* They remained in service until about 1917.

Sagadahoc was a side-wheel steamboat with a vertical beam engine that developed 700 horsepower; it had a single stack and fore and aft sails. The boat was painted all white with dark trimmings, the carved seal of the State of Maine decorating the center of a fan-shaped design on the paddle wheel boxes. Signal letters were H. A. N. M.

The *Sagadahoc* was 244 feet long, 35 feet breadth, 12 feet depth of hold; 1,413 gross tons and 1,266 net tons.

Cumberland

Built in 1885
Captain John Thompson of Eastport, Maine
Captain Hilyard

The *Cumberland* was built at Bath, Maine, in 1885, for the International Steamship Company's Boston-Bangor line. Somewhat larger than the *State of Maine II,* it was used on the Boston-Portland run as well as on the Portland-Bangor-Machias run and made some through trips to St. John, New Brunswick. *Cumberland* was registered at Eastport in 1898.

This portrait by Antonio Jacobsen shows the side-wheel steamboat with a vertical beam engine, twin stacks, two masts and sails.

The *Cumberland* was sold to the Joy Line in 1902 and the name changed to *Larchmont.* On the night of February 11, 1907, the *Larchmont* was in collision with a heavily laden coal schooner off Block Island. Of the one hundred and seventy-seven passengers on board, only seventeen were saved. Signal letters were K. C. W. L.

The *Cumberland* was 252 feet long, 37 feet breadth, 14 feet depth of hold; 1,605 gross tons and 896 net tons.

Steamship   *Long fellow*
Built in 1883
Captain J. Smith

The *Longfellow* was built by the Lockwood Company at East Boston in 1883 expressly for the Boston-Provincetown route. This well-known wooden propeller steamboat ran for many years, sometimes all winter; but while an excellent sea boat, it was designed principally for freight and so was not especially comfortable for passengers.

Both the *Shattuck* and the *Longfellow* sometimes towed vessels, much to the discomfort of their passengers, as this slow action added to the length and tedium of the passage to and from Provincetown.

At one time the *Longfellow* ran between Bucksport, Maine, and Nova Scotia ports. On December 27, 1888, the *Boston Advertiser* announced that the ship would run a sixty-day excursion from Boston to the West Indies, passengers being limited to twenty-five persons. This was one of the earliest advertisements for the winter cruises that are now so popular.

The *Longfellow* was 146 feet long, 27 feet breadth; 413 gross tons and 218 net tons.

Steamboat   # *Tremont*

Built in 1883
Captain John Thompson of Eastport, Maine

The *Tremont* was built at Brooklyn, New York, by John Englis Company in 1883 for the International Steamship Company of Maine, for service from Boston to Portland.

This portrait by Antonio Jacobsen shows the *Tremont* to be a side-wheel boat with a so-called walking beam engine. The construction was all wood, oak and pine.

In 1900 the boat was sold to a New York company and placed in service from New York to Providence.

The *Tremont* was 270 feet long, 37 feet breadth, 12½ feet depth of hold; 1,427 gross tons and 1,023 net tons.

Steamship *Dirigo*

Built in 1865
Captain Charles Johnson
Captain H. Sheerwood

The *Dirigo* was built in 1865 at Portland, Maine, for H. B. Cromwell & Company, especially for the Portland-New York service. The name "Dirigo" meaning "I lead," was taken from the motto used in the seal of the State of Maine.

This interesting portrait shows the small but seaworthy wooden propeller boat with fore and aft sails, at a time when steam was still not wholly trusted. It had an invertible upright triple screw engine.

The *Dirigo* was 184 feet long,
31 feet breadth, 13 feet depth of hold.

Mount Desert

Launched in April, 1879
Captain D. Robinson, 1879-1885

Shown paddling toward Rockland off the southwestern coast of Mount Desert Island, Maine, the steamboat *Mount Desert* was built by Goss & Sawyer Company at Bath, Maine, in 1879, for the Rockland, Mount Desert, and Sullivan Steamboat Company; it was registered at Rockland, Maine. This steamboat was built with an open foredeck, a beam engine of 500 horsepower; and a fan-shaped pattern decorated the paddle wheel boxes. The boat was often referred to as the "Old Mounty" and it had a whistle of a most delightful mellow tone.

The first trip from Rockland, Maine, through the Fox Island Thoroughfare to Bar Harbor and Sullivan was made on June 19, 1879, taking about one hundred and fifty passengers to Bar Harbor; the boat tied up and stayed overnight at Sullivan on its maiden voyage. Steamboat *Catherine* was sometimes used on the Bar Harbor-Rockland Line during the winter months, a small propeller boat being suitable for winter weather.

In 1904, the "Old Mounty" was replaced by the steamboat *J. T. Morse* on the Rockland-Bar Harbor run, and in 1906, was registered at Bath, Maine; it made excursion trips for a short time in Boston Harbor from Nahant, Massachusetts, and soon after was sold to a New York company which changed the name in 1910 to *Arion*. The *Arion* paddled up the Hudson River and to Glen Island until it was condemned in 1913 and broken up in 1914 at Edgewater, New Jersey, on the Hudson River opposite Riverside Drive, New York.

The *Mount Desert* was 163 feet long, 27 feet breadth, 9 feet depth of hold; 457 gross tons and 283 net tons.

Steamboat   *Kennebec III*

Built in 1889
Captain Jason Collins

The *Kennebec III* was built by the New England Shipbuilding Company at Bath, Maine, in 1889, at the time when steamboats were the most popular and convenient way to travel.

This side-wheel boat with a vertical beam engine was constructed entirely of wood. The boilers were placed on the main deck instead of in the hold, which made the *Kennebec III* top-heavy, and as a result it rolled more than was necessary.

After years of service the vessel was sold to a New York company, renamed the *Iroquois,* and placed on the Hudson River Line.

The *Kennebec III* was 256 feet long, 37½ feet beam, 13 feet depth of hold; 1,652 gross tons and 1,271 net tons.

161

Cottage City and Manhattan

Built in 1890   Built in 1891
Captain Bennett   Captain Bragg

The *Cottage City* and the *Manhattan* were sister ships built in 1890-91 by the New England Shipbuilding Company, of Bath, Maine. They had triple expansion engines with cylinders 22, 34 and 56 inches in diameter, by 36 inches stroke.

It was with these new boats that the Maine Steamship Company came to be known as the best-paying coastwise run out of New York.

The *Cottage City* was sold to the Pacific Coast Steamship Company and afterward lost. This is an Antonio Jacobsen painting of the ship.

The *Manhattan* continued as a spare boat, making regular runs in winter, and extra runs in summer. It was discovered to be afire while approaching Franklin Wharf, Portland, on March 10, 1910, and the tugs *Hunnybrooks* and *Portland* towed the burning hull to the South Portland flats. Unfortunately for the owners, the *Manhattan* had been sold for future delivery for $150,000.00 and was carrying only $100,-000.00 insurance. The wreck was sold in Boston for $4,306.00.

The *Cottage City* was 233½ feet in length, 40½ feet beam, 24½ feet depth of hold; 1,892 tons.

The Portland

Built in 1890
Captain H. H. Blanchard

The *Portland II* by name, the sister ship of the *Bay State* though slightly different in size, was built by the New England Shipbuilding Company at Bath, Maine, in 1890. It was the second by the same name to be placed in service from Boston to Portland. The signal letters were K. H. D. R.

As may be seen from this fine portrait by Antonio Jacobsen, the *Portland* was an impressive and beautifully designed boat with a beam engine, twin stacks, and fore and aft sails. The State of Maine seal, carved and polychromed, was placed at the top of each paddle wheel box. A handsome carved and gilded eagle gleamed from the pilot house. The accommodations were considered excellent at that time.

The *Portland II* was wrecked off Cape Cod in the terrible northeast storm of November 26, 1898. Much has been written about this frightful disaster, the worst ever known on the New England Coast, in which all of the passengers and crew, numbering one hundred and seventy-six persons, were lost. It was later considered an Act of God which revolutionized the design of steamboats for ocean use.

The paddle wheel steamboats were no longer considered suitable for ocean-going boats. The fore and aft sails would have been little or no use in such a storm. The theory that the beam engine or rudder gave way is as logical as any, otherwise the boat would have been able to paddle into a sheltering harbor. Also, if there had been a strong and powerful searchlight placed on the pilot house instead of the eagle, it might have been of some help in steering the boat to shelter, even though paddle wheels were sometimes quite useless in heavy seas.

Captain Blanchard was a person of very strong will and determination and is said to have made the decision to sail from Boston on the fatal trip. The *Bay State,* one of the three boats sailing in opposition from Boston to Eastport, Maine, and St. John, New Brunswick, stayed safely in Portland Harbor that night, and the *State of Maine* remained tied up at the wharf in Boston.

The *Portland II* was 280 feet in length,
42 feet beam, 15 feet depth of hold;
2,283 gross tons and 1,517 net tons.

Bangor, Maine

This is a view of the Penobscot River and harbor at Bangor in 1890. It is obvious that the port, now almost dead, was then a very busy place, being the second largest lumber mart of the world.

The harbor was deep enough to float large ships and schooners, even though it was sixty miles up the Penobscot from the sea. Bucksport and Winterport were the navigable ports during the winter months.

This photograph was taken when sails, rails, and steamboats were all still in use. The four-masted schooner at the right is the *Annie E. J. Morse,* built at Bath, Maine, in 1886. Also to be seen are the steamship *Naprima* on its maiden voyage from Newcastle, England, and the handsome iron barque *Dundee,* which was built in Glasgow in 1882.

The large side-wheel steamboat seen in the left background is the *Katahdin.*

Steamboat   *Frank Jones*
Built in 1892

The *Frank Jones* was built by the New England Shipbuilding Company at Bath, Maine, for the Maine Central Railroad in 1892, for service to the most eastern bays and harbors of the Maine coast, including Castine, where this splendid photograph was taken.

It was considered a very modern steamboat at that time and most successful though it had quite an ocean roll. Well designed, with a beautiful saloon and comfortable staterooms, the *Frank Jones* was one of the first large boats on the Maine coast with the incline type of engine, though the beam engine continued to be used on most boats until the loss of the *Portland*. The *Jones* had especially fine life-saving equipment, and a handsome carved and gilded eagle gleamed from the top of the pilot house before searchlights came into use. It carried a crew of forty-nine men.

After thirteen years of service, the vessel was sold and the name changed to *Fenimore*. It was then used on one of the steamboat lines from New York to Fall River, and later was in service on the Hudson River.

In 1917, the *Fenimore* went into war service for the United States Navy and paddled between New York and Norfolk, Virginia. It was blown up while at anchor in the York River.

The *Frank Jones* was 253 feet long,
36 feet breadth, 13 feet depth of hold;
1,634 gross tons and 1,078 net tons.

Steamboat

Vinal Haven
Built in 1892

The *Vinal Haven* was the only steamboat to be built at the seaport town of Searsport, Maine, and was registered at Rockland, Maine, the home port.

This steamboat was one of the lovely sights of Rockland Harbor in the days of real steamboating. Many other small boats traversed the harbor to go out to Swans Island, but none was quite so pleasing as this one.

The *Vinal Haven* was a real propeller steamboat and was nicely designed. Her engine developed 135 horsepower, and she had a crew of six men.

The cabins were small but adequate and comfortable for the times; the open foredeck was used for freight. This steamer continued in service until it was necessary to have a larger boat which could transport automobiles from Rockland to Vinal Haven Island.

The *Vinal Haven* was 100 feet long, 16 feet breadth, 7½ feet depth of hold; 180 gross tons and 126 net tons.

Steamboat　　　　*Catherine*

Built in 1893
Captain Nixon

The *Catherine* was built at Bath, Maine, in 1893, for the Rockland and Blue Hill Steamboat Company. The engines developed 130 horsepower and the boat carried a crew of ten while on the Rockland to Blue Hill run for several years, and later while in service from Bath to Boothbay Harbor.

The steamers *Westport* and *Southport* came from the Bath-Boothbay run to Rockland, and the *Catherine* was transferred to Boston in 1920. At that time the name was changed to *Nahant,* and this steamboat was placed on the Boston-Nahant run.

One summer the *Nahant* ran from Boston to Gloucester, and in 1928 was again sold to New York parties, and ended its days in New York Harbor on the Statue of Liberty run.

This photograph was taken from the steamship *Cimbria,* a Bangor to Bar Harbor steamer with which the *Catherine* was racing at the time, northward bound toward Castine. Cape Rosier is shown in the background.

An upper forward deck was built over the bow to cover freight storage before leaving for Boston in 1920. The mast poles were removed, but the pilot house, flag pole, and smokestack remained the same.

The *Catherine* was 100 feet long,
18 feet breadth, 8 feet depth of hold;
161 tons.

173

Steamboat

City of Bangor
Built in 1894
Captain Ingraham

The *City of Bangor* was built for the Boston & Bangor Steamship Company at Boston, Massachusetts, in 1894, and was registered at Bath, Maine.

This side-wheel boat, operated by a crew of ninety-nine men, had an indicated horsepower of 1,600, and is said to have been used on three different lines for the Maine coast run.

The *City of Bangor* caught fire at Foster's Wharf, in Boston, and was very badly damaged. It was rebuilt like a floating tenement house, which may be seen from this lithograph by Forbes Company, Chelsea.

Steamboat travellers were skeptical of going anywhere on the all-wood side-wheel steamboats after the fire—which could have happened any time while paddling down the coast—and the fateful disaster of the *Portland* which was always in mind. Finally this vessel was tied up and abandoned at East Boston.

> The *City of Bangor* was 277 feet in length, 38 feet breadth, 14 feet depth of hold; 1,661 gross tons and 1,113 net tons.

Steamship   *Governor Dingley*

Built in 1899

Captains: Joseph Brown
    John Thompson, Eastport, Maine   Walter E. Scott
    Ernest Clark   Pilot: Foran

The *Governor Dingley,* named for the twenty-sixth Governor of Maine, Nelson Dingley, Jr., was the first steel hull propeller steamship to be placed in regular Down East service for both passengers and freight. *The Dingley,* as this steamship was often called, was built by The Delaware Shipbuilding Company on the Delaware River for the Portland Steam Packet Company. First registered at Portland, then in service from Boston to Portland, it was later registered at Bath and in service as far as St. John, New Brunswick.

The design and construction of this ship was that of a small ocean liner, which was an assurance to passengers of a fast and safe passage to Down East points, as the disaster of the wooden side-wheel steamboat *Portland* remained vividly in the minds of all steamboat and steamship passengers.

The *Dingley* was built with triple expansion engines of 2,500 horsepower, four boilers which were later converted for oil burning, and cylinders of 23½, 44½, and 70 inches in diameter with 36-inch stroke. This vessel made a speed of fifteen knots; its fastest trip from Boston to Portland is said to have been made in five hours and fifty-five minutes. The crew consisted of seventy-four persons. The signal letters were K. P. L. G.

This steamship was considered very handsome, being painted all white; its saloon, gallery deck, cabins, and 194 staterooms were simply panelled, nicely carpeted and comfortably furnished. The dining room on the lower deck was pleasing and well lighted, not having any of the lavish elegance of the Fall River Line steamers, but a simplicity and style of its own.

In 1901, the Portland Steam Packet Company merged in with the Eastern Steamship Company of Maine, and later built two other steel-hull seaworthy steamships, similar in design, the *Governor Cobb* and the *Calvin Austin.* They were placed in alternating service, sometimes stopping at the ports of Rockland, Camden, Belfast, then way on Down East to Eastport, Lubec, and St. John.

Unfortunately the steel hull of the *Dingley* was so designed that the vessel rolled continuously in an ocean swell, even when fully loaded

with a cargo of sardines or dried cod from Eastport and Lubec, or with other freight from St. John.

Regardless of its rocking, voyages on the *Dingley* were always worth while, as the distant view of the coast of Maine, New Brunswick, their islands and ports from the hurricane deck was a magnificent and well-remembered scene. A heavy fog would sometimes veil this scenery during part of the trip, but would gradually disappear, revealing a scene of magic beauty.

This portrait by Antonio Jacobsen is most realistic, the drawing accurate and interesting. Jacobsen often painted several portraits of the same ship, and a duplicate of this painting may be seen at the Portland Marine Society, Portland, Maine.

The *Governor Dingley* once encountered a most severe northeast storm on one of the winter passages from Boston to Portland. Two of the steel shutters on the forward part of the ship became damaged, and the crew had to pile part of the cargo against them to keep the overpowering and frigid waves from sinking the ship, as the freight or lower deck had become flooded. The network and railing around the hurricane and promenade decks were a solid block of ice, as well as the bow of the boat, where two bow watchers were keeping alert though they were nearly frozen. Fortunately the ship, which was pitching and rolling badly, was commanded by two very skillful men. Pilot Foran's grim fortitude and perseverance in keeping his head out of the pilot house window, and the help of his two heroic bow watchers enabled the *Dingley* to make Portland Harbor safely and disembark all passengers. It is doubtful whether a wooden side-wheel beam engine boat would have been able to survive such a rough storm and battering in midwinter.

Another interesting episode in the career of the *Dingley* while in Maine coastal waters and before the days of radar equipment, happened when the keen ears of the bow watcher heard the signal of an approaching schooner, the *Annie and Reuben,* during a very dense fog; the Captain slowed the ship and put the engines in reverse, the steamship safely passed the schooner within a few yards unseen, so near that voices could be heard clearly from the schooner, which was commanded by Captain Perry.

The *Governor Dingley* was purchased by the United States Government for a training ship in 1917, and dismantled at Baltimore in 1933.

> The *Governor Dingley* was 324 feet long, 62 feet breadth, 17 feet depth of hold; 3,826 gross tons and 2,856 net tons.

Steamship   # Horatio Hall

Built in 1898
Captain D. Wallace
Captain Albert Bragg

The *Horatio Hall* was built by the Delaware River Shipbuilding Company, at Chester, Pennsylvania, for the Maine Steamship Company whose ships sailed from Portland to Cottage City and New York City. This ship, named for Captain Horatio Hall, a native of Harpswell, Maine, was placed in alternating service with the steamship *John Englis* for a time, until the latter was chartered by the United States Government and used as a relief ship during the Spanish American War. The *Horatio Hall* and the *John Englis,* built in 1896, were considered twin ships, though slightly different in size. The *Hall* was most successful on the New York-Portland run, making the 390-mile trip in twenty-two hours. These handsome steamships were built with steel hulls, painted black, three upper decks painted white, fore and aft masts with sails, and one stack; each steamer was equipped with 4,200 horsepower engines, and the passenger accommodations were very fine; the dining saloon on the upper deck was most attractive.

On March 9, 1909, the *Horatio Hall,* while bound for New York, was sunk in a collision with the steamer *H. F. Dimock* which was headed eastward during a dense fog while passing through Pollock Rip Slue, south of Monomoy Point, Chatham, Massachusetts. The *Hall* sank quickly, but the *Dimock,* a smaller steamer, remained afloat after the accident, stood by, and rescued all the *Hall's* passengers and crew, then steamed fifteen miles to Nauset Beach where it made a landing and disembarked all the passengers, who arrived safely at their ultimate destinations. The *Dimock* was repaired, refloated, and later taken to Boston where it was put back into first-class condition. Because the Pollock Rip Slue is such a narrow channel between the numerous shoals south of Monomoy Point and north of Great Point, Nantucket Island, there was not enough passageway clear of the *Horatio Hall's* sunken hull to allow another steamer to pass at low tide; the U. S. Government abandoned its plans of raising the *Hall* and in due time set charges of dynamite and blew up the steamship. Signal letters of the *Hall* were K. N. J. L. This portrait was painted by Jacobsen.

The *Horatio Hall* was 296 feet long, 46 feet breadth, 17 feet depth of hold; 3,169 gross tons and 2,007 net tons.

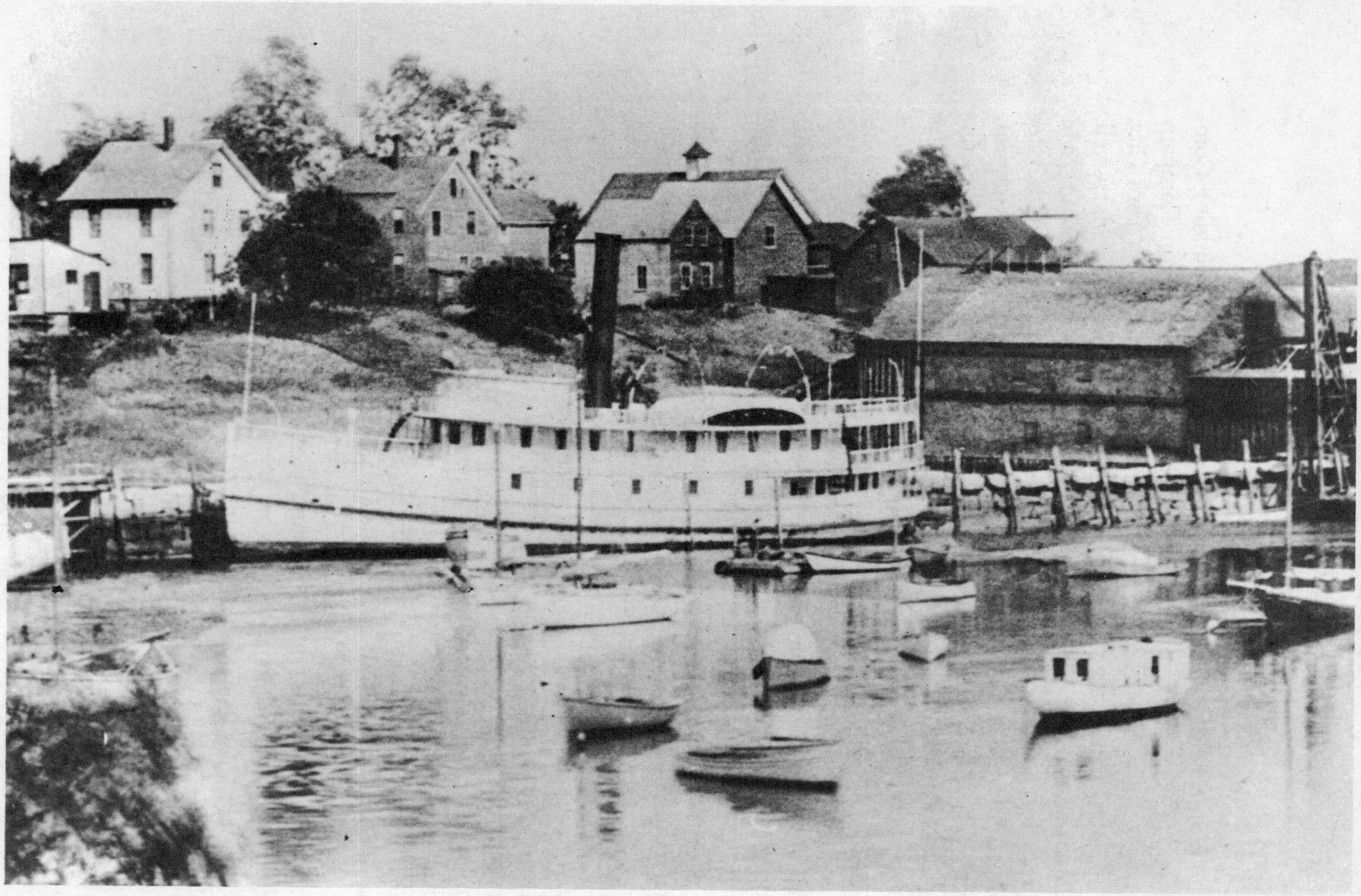

From the Authors' Collection

Henry F. Eaton

Built in 1901
Captain George Waite

The *Henry F. Eaton* was built at South Portland, Maine, in 1901, for the Frontier Steamboat Company of Calais, Maine, for the Triangular Service from Eastport to Calais and St. Andrews. It carried both freight and passengers and connected with the Boston and St. John boats at Eastport.

This staunch boat was said to have been the strongest little steamer built in the state, and was named for a member of a well-known family of Calais, Maine. There is a story that the namesake objected to having his name used for the *Henry F. Eaton,* and that apparently the steamer also objected strenuously, as it behaved very badly until its name was changed, being involved in a series of accidents on the St. Croix River.

Once it crashed into a pile of lumber on the Canadian side of the river near St. Stephen during a foggy night; the next morning the townspeople were astounded to see the *Eaton* with its nose poked into a vast lumber pile, with stray pieces of wood straddling its decks. After the tide receded, the steamer was left with about two-thirds of its length wedged into a mountain of cut timber, the stern resting on the beach and the propeller ready to twirl in midair. On the next tide the boat was pulled out uninjured, and by the following day was making its regular trips down the river. Having been so strongly built the collision with the lumber pile caused little or no damage.

On another occasion the *Eaton* took some townspeople on a gala picnic excursion to Hill's Point on the Canadian shore. While the Captain lingered overtime with picnic merrymaking along the Wa Weig River, the tide dropped twenty-three or more feet, and when the party returned the rugged little *Eaton* was found resting high and dry on a mammoth long ledge, where it had to remain until the next morning. The stranded picnickers were obliged to sit out all night on the shore until the sunrise tide refloated the boat. The grounding damaged the vessel very slightly, for it was steaming the river proudly again the next day.

Another untimely accident happened when the *Eaton* ran ashore in the fog at Deer Island and struck a rock; the captain realized it would be impossible to hold his steamer ashore long enough to land his passengers, so he signalled full speed astern, wheeled the steamer around and headed immediately for the American side of the river. The vessel filled rapidly, but Captain Waite managed to beach the steamer just in time, for the saloon deck had already been submerged and the passengers were huddled around the life rafts on the hurricane deck. All were taken off safely, however. The next day the hull was patched, the boat was towed to Calais for further repairs, and it was soon placed in regular service again.

Upon being sold to the Eastern Steamship Company the name was changed to *St. Andrews*. As soon as the name was changed this steamer seemed to discontinue its misbehavior and wild adventures.

The *St. Andrews* continued in service until purchased by the United States Government in 1917. After serving the St. Croix region for about fifteen years, it steamed along the coast to Camden, Maine, where this characteristic portrait was made. It was tied up there for about five years and was later resold to New York interests for service on the Hudson River.

This steamer had a turbine engine of 300 horsepower, and was manned by a crew of twelve.

> The *Henry F. Eaton* was 113 feet long, 27 feet breadth, 19 feet depth of hold; 240 gross tons, and 141 net tons.

Steamboat

City of Rockland
Built in 1901
Captain Otis Ingraham

The *City of Rockland,* built by James McKie at East Boston, Massachusetts, in 1901, and registered at Bath, Maine, was an all wood side-wheel boat painted white, with fore and aft masts, a single stack, and a cased-in beam engine of 1,600 horsepower; the saloon was most elaborate. This boat had accommodations for 600 overnight passengers as well as a 600 ton freight capacity. Though the *City of Rockland* was constructed with a single stack, it was considered the sister ship of the *City of Bangor,* which had two stacks placed sidewise, but was about the same size and overall design.

In 1904, this steamboat ran onto a ledge near Rockland in a dense fog; it was hauled off, repaired, and placed in service again. In 1912, it was in collision with the collier, *William Chism,* near Boon Island in another dense fog; it was hauled away and towed to Boston for repairs. However, as reconstruction of the old wooden side-wheel boats was considered impractical, the boat was sold to wreckers in 1924 and later towed to Little Misery Island, near Beverly, Mass., and burned.

The signal letters of the *Rockland* were K. Q. W. G. This portrait is after the painting by Antonio Jacobsen.

> The *City of Rockland* was 274 feet long, 38 feet in breadth, 14 feet depth of hold; 1,696 gross tons and 1,026 net tons.

183

From the Stebbins Collection, Harrison Gray Otis House, Boston

J. T. Morse

Built in 1904
Captain F. L. Winterbotham
Captain Addison Schute
Captain Hardy D. Schute

The *J. T. Morse,* named for one of the Morse Steamboat Company, was built at East Boston, Massachusetts, in 1904, for the Rockland-Bar Harbor Line, and registered at Bath. This side-wheel steamboat was nicely designed, with fore and aft masts, a single stack, and a beam engine of 600 horsepower; the paddle wheel boxes were plain. The walking beam was painted white at one time, which added to the beauty of this boat.

The *Morse* was in passenger and freight service during the summer months from Rockland to the various islands of Penobscot Bay, South Blue Hill, Mount Desert Island and Sullivan; sometimes it made special trips to Eastport or to Portland. The *Morse* was considered fast, making 16½ knots on long trips.

While in Down East service the *Morse* was involved in a series of accidents which caused much excitement and interest during steamboat days. Twice the boat was sunk, raised, and again placed in service. From November until April of each year, the *Morse* was tied up at Camden until sold to New York interests in 1933. The boat was somewhat rebuilt at that time and the name changed to *Yankee;* it was then used as an excursion steamer on several different runs in New York Harbor until condemned in 1941. The *Morse* had a crew of twenty-seven men while in Down East service; signal letters were K. T. D. P.

The *J. T. Morse* was 199 feet long,
31 feet breadth, 12 feet depth of hold;
780 gross tons and 410 net tons.

Steamship   *Governor Cobb*

Built in 1906
Captain John Thompson
Captain Winchester
Captain Pike

In 1901, when the International Steamship Company joined with the Morse Eastern Steamship Company, consolidating all the lines running eastward from Boston, they added to their fleet by building two more steel hull propeller steamships, the *Calvin Austin,* in 1903, and the *Governor Cobb,* to be placed in alternating service with the *Governor Dingley,* from Boston to Eastport, Lubec, and St. John. These two new steamships were built by the Delaware River Shipbuilding Company at Chester, Pennsylvania, and registered at Bath, Maine; they were rated two of the fastest and most successful ships used on the Maine coast run. Equipped with triple turbine engines of 2,500 horsepower each, they had comfortable staterooms and attractive saloons. Fortunately, neither the *Cobb* nor the *Austin* had the terrific roll of the *Governor Dingley* while making an ocean voyage. The *Governor Cobb* was named for William Titcomb Cobb of Rockland, Maine, who served the Executive Council of the State of Maine and was twice elected Governor of Maine, in 1904 and 1906. This ship was the first real seagoing steamship built in the United States which was powered with triple turbine machinery.

During the winter months the *Calvin Austin* and *Governor Cobb* were used on the run between Key West and Havana; their hulls were painted black temporarily, with upper decks white, while serving this popular route.

In the first World War, these steamships, along with the *Governor Dingley,* were taken over by the United States Government for war service.

The *Governor Cobb* proved its serviceability and usefulness when it was again taken for war service during World War II. The signal letters were K. V. Q. J.

The *Governor Cobb* was 289 feet long, 54 feet breadth, 18 feet depth of hold; 2,552 gross tons and 1,556 net tons.

Steamship   *Bunker Hill*

Built in 1907
Captain J. Healy

In 1907, the Maine Steamship Company, sometimes called the Merchants' Line, built three steamships, the *Massachusetts, Bunker Hill,* and the *Old Colony,* thus making an effort to establish direct steamship connection for freight from New York to Portland and Rockland, Maine; the latter place was formerly the steamboat terminal city of Down East, having fifteen different steamboat connections at one time.

These new steamships were built by Cramp & Company of Philadelphia, all three being very nearly the same size; the *Bunker Hill* and the *Massachusetts* were each constructed with twin turbine engines and the *Old Colony* was equipped with triple turbine engines; all three of these steamships were first registered at Portland. In 1912, these ships were rebuilt for passenger service as well as freight, the first two being converted to oil burners. The *Bunker Hill* and the *Massachusetts* were placed in alternating service from Boston to New York. The *Old Colony* remained in service from New York to Portland until taken by the United States Government.

After the opening of the Cape Cod Canal these steamships used it regularly, avoiding many of the dangers of navigating around Cape Cod, and also reducing the distance from New York to Boston some 260 miles. The *Massachusetts* and the *Bunker Hill* ran regularly on this route until November of 1917, at which time they were purchased by the United States Government; then being rebuilt and renamed *Shawmut* and *Aroostook,* they were used most successfully as mine layers and were permanently retained by the U. S. Navy. Signal letters of the *Bunker Hill* were K. V. D. T. This portrait was painted by Antonio Jacobsen.

> The *Bunker Hill* was 375 feet long, 52 feet breadth, 30 feet depth of hold; 4,799 gross tons and 2,575 net tons.

Courtesy of Mariners' Museum, Newport News, Va.

Camden and Belfast

Built in 1907
Captain George W. Sawyer
Captain A. E. Rawley
Captain Ezra W. Curtis
Captain Strickland

The *Camden* was built at Bath, Maine, in 1907, for the Eastern Steamship Company and was named for the beautiful seaport town on Penobscot Bay where "Down East" really begins. This steamship was one of two handsome seaworthy ships of the same design and dimensions, each being slightly different in tonnage; the second ship was also built at Bath, in 1909, and named *Belfast* after another beautiful seaport town on Penobscot Bay. These towns were used regularly as ports of call by both ships.

These popular steamships were usually thought of as "The Twins" and were often called sister ships; when either one was mentioned the other immediately came to mind as it was impossible to discuss one without referring to the other.

Both of these ships were exceptionally well built with strong steel hulls, triple turbine engines of 4,000 horsepower, twin stacks, fore and aft masts; and were painted white all over. The saloon, cabins and staterooms were nicely panelled, simply decorated, and comfortably furnished, and the dining rooms were inviting and attractive as well. These steamships were also distinguished for the pleasant tone of their whistles, which were most delightful to hear.

The *Camden* and the *Belfast* were first placed in service from Boston to Bangor, and sometimes made trips way down east as far as St. John, New Brunswick. They were very fast; both ships often made three round trips a week from Boston to Bangor.

In 1918, they were taken for service on the Metropolitan Line going from Boston to New York, by way of the Cape Cod Canal. They left

Boston at India Wharf, and arrived and departed from Pier 18 at the foot of Murray Street, New York.

In 1925, the *Camden* and the *Belfast* were again placed in Down East service upon the completion of the steamships *Boston* and *New York*. In 1935 they were purchased for the Colonial Line and put on the Providence-New York route. As they thus made a permanent departure from Maine coastal waters their names were changed: the *Camden* became the *Comet,* and the *Belfast* became the *Arrow.*

After a brief service on the Colonial Line, the *Arrow* and the *Comet* were purchased by the United States Government and entirely rebuilt for war service in the Pacific. The steel hulls and engines remained much the same, but these handsome ships could hardly be identified after the reconstruction was completed. They were in use in the Hawaiian Islands throughout the war.

These ships were again sold for freight service on the West Coast. The *Comet* later was sent to China to be used as a troopship along the Yangtse Kiang River during the Korean War, and since then has been taken over by the Chinese Communist Government. The *Arrow,* renamed *Argus,* was wrecked on the Washington coast in 1947.

These steamships each had a crew of one hundred twenty persons while in New England coastal service; the *Camden's* signal letters were K. W. C. G.; the *Belfast's* signal letters were L. B. C. Q.

The *Camden* was 320 feet long, 40 feet breadth, 16 feet depth of hold; 2,153 gross tons and 1,143 net tons.

The *Belfast* was 320 feet long, 40 feet breadth, 16 feet depth of hold; 2,157 gross tons and 1,147 net tons.

Steamship
Rangeley
Built in 1913
Captain Archibald

The *Rangeley* was one of two small steel hull steamships built at Bath, Maine, for the Maine Central Railroad Company, which operated them across Frenchman's Bay from Mt. Desert Ferry in Hancock, Maine, to Bar Harbor, Seal Harbor, and Southwest Harbor. Other well-known steamers used on this so-called "Round the Hills Service" were the *Moosehead, Sappho, Norumbega,* and the *Sebenoa.* The *Rangeley,* equipped with a 1,200 horsepower engine, was a luxury ship compared to the old steamers, and proved to be the fastest ship to travel at any time on the "Round the Hills Service." This splendid photograph was taken during the *Rangeley's* service along the Maine coast.

In 1925, this steamship was sold to the Hudson River Day Line, and its name was changed to *Chauncey M. Depew*. In 1941, it was chartered by the United States Government. After the war, the *Chauncey M. Depew* was again sold and placed on the Boston-Provincetown Line for several years until this line was taken over by a Baltimore company. This steamship was then placed in service at Bermuda. The signal letters were L. D. B. G.

The *Rangeley* was 185 feet long,
35 feet breadth, 13 feet depth of hold;
652 gross tons and 282 net tons.

193

Twin Steamships *Yarmouth and Evangeline*
Built in 1927

In the summer of 1927, the handsome new steamships *Yarmouth* and *Evangeline* made their first appearance across the Gulf of Maine, from the shipbuilding yards of W. Cramp & Sons Company, of Philadelphia. These fine ships were considered de luxe liners with accommodations for 750 first-class passengers and 33 special de luxe cabins; the freight deck was designed with automobile holds so that one could drive a car on board at Boston and off again at Yarmouth.

These twin steamships were each built with steel hulls painted black, three upper decks painted white, fore and aft masts, a single stack; and equipped with twin propeller turbine-driven oil burning engines.

The *Yarmouth* and the *Evangeline* followed the smart steamships *Prince George* and *Prince Arthur* on this famous Land of Evangeline Cruise. The *S. S. Evangeline* was the last steamship to cross the Gulf of Maine to the Maritime Provinces in 1954, and was finally sold for service on the Florida coast; it steamed out of Boston Harbor for the last time in the spring of 1955.

There are only about three steamboats now traversing Boston Harbor during the summer months, and only a few Island Steamers are left along the Maine and New Brunswick coast. The Eastern Steamship Service to St. John terminated in 1935.

The signal letters of the *Yarmouth* were M. G. N. D.; those of the *Evangeline* were M. G. N. P.

The *Yarmouth* was 365 feet long,
55 feet breadth, 26 feet depth of hold;
5,043 gross tons and 2,714 net tons.

195

APPENDIX

PAINTERS OF THE STEAMBOATS

FRED PANSING
Very little is known of the painter Fred Pansing. It is said that he was born in Scotland and painted many of the Cunard Line steamships before coming to this country. He painted many of the Canadian Pacific Railway Company steamships and Fall River Line steamboats, as well as the Boston Harbor boats. His works are not only realistic, accurate, and exquisite, but are masterpieces of marine painting. Reproduced in this volume are his pictures of the *Eagle, Lafayette,* and the *Rose Standish.*

Several of his paintings are owned by the New York Historical Society and the Fall River Historical Society, and many are in private collections throughout the country. New York directories list him from 1897 to 1905 as an artist, at 218 Fulton Street; his home was at 124 Sip Avenue, Jersey City.

ANTONIO NICOLO GASPARO JACOBSEN
Antonio Nicolo Gasparo Jacobsen, son of a long line of makers of fine violins in Denmark, was born in Copenhagen on November 2, 1850.

Ole Bull, the famous violinist, a friend of the family who was at the christening, insisted that the child be named after the great violin makers of the world: Antonio after Stradivarius, Nicolo after Amati, and Gasparo after Bartolotti da Salo; hence the unique names for a Danish person.

The family expected him to become a musician, and he did become so sufficiently skilled at playing the violin, viola, and cello that he derived much happiness from his playing late in life. But as a boy he was much more fascinated by ships and the sea, and he later told with much emotion of often watching the great sailing fleet of Denmark enter Copenhagen Harbor under full sail, with billowing canvas, the sun glittering on the blue water, on which floated many of the famous ships of other nations riding at anchor. As a small boy escaping family vigilance, he haunted the quays, spending all his spare time and allowance hiring small boats in order to study and observe more closely these ships at anchor; he would go on board them, plying everyone with countless questions. Years after, he was immensely proud of the accuracy of his nautical observations as shown in his steamship paintings, of every line, block, and pulley—any experienced seaman could scrutinize them and find no technical fault in evidence. He often said with a twinkle, that he was "not an artist, but a painter of floating property—ships' portraits."

At the outbreak of the Franco-Prussian War in 1870, the Jacobsen family fortunes waned. At that time all large houses in Denmark were arranged in such a way that there were frequently shops on the ground floor, maybe a count or a baron living on the next above, the owners on the third floor, and so on along the social scale, until the top floor or garret was occupied by students and servants. When the government quartered ten soldiers on the Jacobsen family to be housed and fed, all these paying people had to be asked to leave. As in every war, cultural and constructive activities were stopped and business was ruined. Art student Antonio Jacobsen was obliged to give up his studies, leave the Royal Academy of Design where he had been studying, and take a business position in a great commercial house of Copenhagen.

From a picturesque repertoire of stories about his home in the old country, Antonio later told how in summers his family visited their uncle who was chief steward at the Royal Palace and lived in a cottage on the grounds of the Summer Palace—a vast and beautiful park called Sorginfru, "Sorrowfree." Every afternoon at three o'clock the Queen, riding in her shining coach, drawn by six black horses, with coachmen, footmen, outriders thundering ahead, all in livery, drove through the park in great splendor. Often, while out walking with their mother, the Jacobsens met the royal cavalcade, and they bowed deeply in awe and reverence. After his death the uncle lay in state within the Royal Palace, an immense honor.

Occasionally the Jacobsens were invited to the Royal Palace for afternoon tea served with delectable little cakes and confections. Sometimes the Queen herself gave them presents, among which were a lovely Sévres vase and an ancient ivory snuff-box with a miniature painting on the lid, still treasured by the family. Antonio told of an unexploded shell dating from the British bombardment of Copenhagen, lodged in the tower of the Church of Saint Nicolas, where formerly the family were permitted to hang their violins in certain stages of drying, high from dust. He told many other delightful stories about his native Denmark and sang with gusto her songs telling of her history and folklore, of her achievements, of her great national heroes.

Like most people of his temperament young Jacobsen loathed all the violent commotion of war and its evil consequences. Feeling that compulsory military training for such a tiny country was absurd, that the vital years of his youthful life would be wasted, at the age of twenty-one, in 1871, he deliberately made a momentous decision—to flee to America. This, of course, was a serious offense, and his share in the family estate was soon confiscated. Many years after, the King returned him his estate.

Antonio told of his unutterably desolate first Christmas Eve alone in New York, a wonderful night of family festivals back home in Denmark where the family gathered about a great tree banked with presents for everybody, and where dancing and singing took place after a tremendous and ceremonious dinner.

In New York, he studied continuously, painted, and went to concerts, lectures, to galleries and museums, reading endlessly, also playing his violin and absorbing much good music.

Soon after his arrival here he was employed by the Marvin Safe Company, to decorate their safe doors. One day an official of the Old Dominion Line, while watching him paint, asked if he could do marine scenes—the thing he preferred to do above all else! This started him on what was to be his life work. Pictures of various steamers of the Old Dominion Line were ordered. This contract was followed by orders for portraits of all the Fall River Line steamboats, including the *Newport, Providence, Metropolis, Massachusetts,* and many others. The company was so pleased with these paintings that he was commissioned to go to Fall River to sketch from life what little was available of their early steamers, the *Bay State* and *State of Maine.* At this time he was completing for the newly organized White Star Line pictures of all their first vessels, the *Oceanic, Celtic, Baltic,* and others. Further orders came to him from the Maine Steamship Company, the Eastern Steamship Company, the Anchor Line, South American Lines, and many ship companies.

On July 6, 1878, Antonio Jacobsen was married to Mary Melanie Schmitt at the Church of the Strangers in New York City. The Fall River Line gave him as a wedding present a trip to Fall River in the bridal suite on the fine new steamer *Bristol.* The honeymoon was spent in and about Fall River and Boston, where his wife, daughter of an Alsatian schoolmaster, had been born and brought up.

In 1880, the Jacobsens moved to West Hoboken, later renamed Union City, New Jersey, into a large house with a lovely garden, huge trees, and flowering shrubs of many varieties. Antonio loved horses and acquired several which he kept in the stable. Here was a magnificent view of the Hudson River and all New York beyond it; Antonio could watch the transatlantic steamships arrive and depart in New York Harbor. He lived happily for a long time, and after twelve years, three children arrived to make him happier still. Their names were Helen, Carl and Alphonse.

Several of Jacobsen's oil paintings hang in the Peabody Museum at Salem, Massachusetts, the Mariners' Museum at Newport News, Virginia, and the New York Historical Society in New York City; many are also in private collections. He loved to say that his pictures could be found any place from a mansion to a tavern, and friends told him often, upon arriving in Europe: "The first thing I saw was one of your paintings!" His paintings are most accurate, exquisite, and decorative. He was probably the first marine artist to do paintings in the mass production style. Sometimes his son and daughter helped him paint on the canvases and boards on which he was hard at work.

Jacobsen knew other marine artists of his day, including S. Ward Stanton, Fred Pansing, who lived nearby in Jersey City, James Bard, the older marine artist whom we have to thank for many examples of early steamboats, Fred Cozzins, and Buttersworth; later, Wood and A. F. Bishop of New Haven, Connecticut.

In 1909, his much loved wife passed on. In 1917, a fire destroyed much of his home. In May of 1918, his two sons were inducted into the United States Army, and the war ruined his business, just as another war had ruined his early family life previously in Denmark. All this darkened his life sadly beyond knowing, and on February 2, 1921, he passed away.

JOHN AND JAMES BARD

The twin brothers John and James Bard were America's foremost self-taught painters of early steamboats. Their work as primitives and historical records is outstanding, decorative and amusing. The portrait of the steamboat *Ocean* by James Bard is reproduced on page 125.

The Bard brothers were born near the village of Chelsea on the Hudson River, New York.

The material which follows is quoted from an article entitled "Primitive Painters in America," by Jean Lipman and Alice Winchester, first published in the April 1949 issue of *Art in America*.

200

Like other primitive artists, the Bard brothers made no pretense at competition with their more academic contemporaries. Their self-appointed task was to depict a given vessel as faithfully as possible. . . . Since their pictures describe better than words the steamboats of their day, they deserve perhaps even greater credit as marine historians.

Yet when James Bard died, only a marine journal noted the fact. An obituary published in the April 1, 1897, issue of *Seaboard* magazine gives the only biographical notes we have of him and his twin brother:

"Mr. James Bard, the last of New York's oldtime marine artists, died at his home in White Plains, New York, on Friday last, March 26, in his 82nd year. . . .

"Mr. Bard was born in 1815, in a little house overlooking the Hudson, in what was then the suburban village of Chelsea; his early home stood on the land which is now bounded by 20th and 21st streets, and 9th and 10th avenues, New York City. His twin brother [John] died in 1856. . . .

"Mr. Bard made his first painting in 1827, finishing in that year a picture of the "Bellona," the first steamboat owned by Commodore Vanderbilt, with whom he was well acquainted. From 1827 to within a few years of his death, Mr. Bard made drawings of almost every steamer that was built or owned around the port of New York, the total number of these productions being about 4,000. Probably Mr. Bard was without a parallel in the faithfulness of delineation in his drawings of vessels. His methods of work, the minuteness of detail, and the absolute truthfulness of every part of a steamboat which characterized his productions, cannot but cause wonder in these days of rapid work. His pictures were always side views, and this often made faulty perspective, yet a Bard picture will ever be held in esteem for its correctness and the beauty of drawing.

"His life work is finished, and the world is richer for it. Were it not for the pictures to be found here and there—and now fast disappearing—we would not know what beautiful specimens of steam vessel architecture our forefathers were capable of turning out. No one in his time compared with James Bard in the matter of making drawings of vessels, and his name will ever be associated with the lists of artists of this country who make a specialty of painting pictures of vessels. In the art he was the father of them all."

The early works were usually signed J. & J. Bard. Over two dozen of the known paintings were done by the two brothers, the latest one being of the steamboat *Wilson G. Hunt,* dated 1849. A few of the pictures signed J. Bard, Painters, also suggest their working together. John Bard's share of the output was, however, of small volume and consequence compared to that of his brother who survived him forty-one years.

In signing most of his work, James Bard usually included his complete address as well, a practical note obviously designed to bring more clients to his door. This serves to inform us that in 1851 and 1852 James Bard was living at 688 Washington Street, and, after 1854, at 162 Perry Street, both in lower Manhattan, appropriately near the downtown docks along the Hudson River. . . .

Bard's pictures of vessels bear so much resemblance to mechanical drawings that it has been conjectured that he might have been a shipyard draftsman, or copied draftmen's work. We know that he frequented the shipyards which constructed the vessels he painted. . . . However, no evidence has been found to show that he was actually employed by the yards as a draftsman, and there are reasons to question the theory that his work was copied.

The characteristics of a James Bard painting are so definite that little skill would be required to recognize an unsigned example. An avoidance of any but the simplest perspective is typical. Never did he attempt a bow or quarter view of a vessel, always picturing the craft from the broadside and, except in some of the earlier works done in collaboration with his brother, almost invariably the port side. Thus his boats steam from right to left and apparently at full speed. None show at anchor or alongside a wharf. In the case of side-wheel vessels, his most common subjects, his point of perspective was usually taken from slightly forward of the paddlebox. Anything in the ship's construction which called for perspective drawing was apparently difficult for him to handle convincingly. When steering wheels show through pilot-house windows, they generally appear as though mounted fore and aft instead of athwartships!

But the most noticeable and perhaps the most charming Bard "hallmark" consists of a unique stippling of the water at the ship's bow. For a considerable area ahead of his vessels, the water seems to bubble like soda water. The same effervescent treatment is seen in the backwash of the paddle wheel and in the ship's wake. . . .

One of the outstanding primitive characteristics of Bard's work is in his handling of the human figure. Odd characters man and travel on his vessels. Whether deck hands or passengers, they almost invariably wear high silk hats and long black frock coats. Occasionally one chances to be normally proportioned, but the majority are grotesque caricatures of men with long bodies and short legs, and some, especially when uninhibited by a deck above, are extraordinarily tall. Nearly

202

all of them seem uncomfortable and decidedly out of place on shipboard. Of female figures there are very few. Bard's later paintings and drawings show but few people, often only the man at the wheel. In some instances, the vessel proceeds up the river completely unattended.